My Pain is My Legacy

BROKEN BUT NOT DAMAGE

By Alexandria Nolan

authorHOUSE®

AuthorHouse™
1663 Liberty Drive
Bloomington, IN 47403
www.authorhouse.com
Phone: 1-800-839-8640

This is a memoir. While inspired by true events and my recollections, they may not coincide with what others depicted in the story experienced or remember. Therefore, in consideration of that fact and in the interest of protecting their privacy, the author has changed names, locations, or situations.

Published by AuthorHouse 9/17/2013

ISBN: 978-1-4918-1214-3 (sc)
ISBN: 978-1-4918-1213-6 (hc)
ISBN: 978-1-4918-1215-0 (e)

Library of Congress Control Number: 2013915222

For we are still the children of our past, just a year older.

This book is dedicated to the following:

Primarily God, for sustaining me and giving me courage
to get through every obstacle set in front of me.

I want to thank everyone that hurt me, because through the
pain, I have become stronger, wiser, and open-minded. I have
become a woman not afraid to tackle anything or anyone.

I want to dedicate this book to all the children who
are hurt, or adults who sustained a lot. I want you to
know I hear you, I feel you, and I love you.

To Oprah Winfrey—for being my number #1 inspiration.
You pushed me when you didn't even know you were. Your
character alone means so much to me. Your story, your strength,
and your journey are the light that leads me to success.

To my children—for being God's gift to me and showing
me unconditional love. You showed me I had another
chance to live life the right way through you.

To my mate—for encouraging me to go forward

And finally yet importantly, to all my true friends and family
members—you know who you are. Thanks for believing in me.

Introduction

At the beginning of this book, I was a thirty-one-year-old single woman and mother. By the end of this book, I am hoping to be an accomplished writer, through with school, and at peace with my inner self.

I have suppressed my inner self for so many years, and now I am ready to let go and let the words flow. I started to write this book before, but I could not quite get it. At this moment in my life, I am discovering peace, and who I am. I am no longer afraid of my inner self or speaking the truth. I am now ready to break down the walls that have darkened my path and shine through.

I know now that people have not because they want not. I want success, so I will go get it. It is now up to me. My life has not been a fairy tale. It has been kind of like a horror movie with a twist. There have been PG-13 rated sections, X-rated sections, and G-rated sections, but you will read and feel it all. So get prepared to share my world. I do not care about hurting anyone's feelings, because I been hurting for over twenty years.

I will now break through the prison walls of my pain. As I write, I am writing off the top of my head. Freedom of speech is beautiful. With so much on TV being reality-based, I guess my book should interest a lot of people because it will be a reality-based book. I will be writing on a day-to-day basis or when I find the time. You all will go through my self-discovery with me.

It is a privilege to have you find an interest in my story, so follow me on my path of self-development, and please learn as you move along.

Let us start with a prayer: Dear God, in the name of the Son, the Father, and the Holy Ghost, in the name of Jesus Christ, please touch me as I write. Allow me to deliver my story in a unique and sufficient way. Please touch the readers and guide me on my path to success.

Chapter 1

My eyes have seen a lot, from light to dark to shades of gray,
from happiness to sadness to just living day by day,
yet my eyes shine so bright awaiting the day
Where the sun will have to wear shades because it has
outdone the sunray.

Here I go starting to write again. Where do I find the words? I have been stuck within myself for so long, I feel like I am missing. Who will gain from the story I have to tell?

Where will it land me emotionally once I allow the surface of my past to unfold? I sometimes feel like a lost soul with no place to go except deep within myself.

A person can hurt the flesh, but he or she cannot take the soul. When I leave the world, I want my soul to live on and my legacy to outweigh my pain.

I guess a purpose so strong is what plays a major part in why I have stayed functionally sane for so long. The only explosion I want in my life is the one where my talent explodes. So that is where my story will begin from my soul.

Today is Tuesday, November 17, 2009, two days from my thirty-first birthday and the first day of the rest of my life. I decided that the other day. Funny how when you look back at your past thoughts for just a second, you only then realize how so much of your life has changed. Well, at least mine has.

I am about to go outside my home and write, while my day-care children are resting.

Writing for me is therapeutic. It allows me to express my deepest emotions without being judged. I love how I can go in a space and console myself with words that flow from my soul. Over the years, writing has become my best friend.

My name is Alex. I am currently the owner of a day care business. I have been running my business for over twelve years now. I enjoy my job and the many children's lives I help to make a difference in. I am now in the position where I want more. I am ready to get on to the next level and grow in my field. My field can get challenging at times, but nothing is more challenging than my life. Hmmm, cut your phone off, get comfortable on the couch, grab a soda, and let me tell you my story.

At this moment, I am a thirty-one-year-old woman, living in the metropolitan area of Washington DC. For those who are unaware of where that is, I live in the DMV, about fifteen minutes from Washington DC, close to Virginia and near Maryland. You know about Washington DC, right? The nation's capital, that is my hometown, but to me, it is not a town to write home about. I have been here my whole life. At this point, I am ready to move. Aside from my grandmother and my job, there is nothing keeping me here. My children can go to whatever school I choose if I move. Oh, sorry, I didn't mention I have three beautiful children.

Yes, I am thirty-one years old with a fourteen-year-old. I've heard it before, but look, I did not allow my age to stop me from being a good parent. I never planned to have children that young. And I definitely never planned to have children by the person I once looked up to as a role model.

When I was young, it seemed like trouble just followed me everywhere. I kind of felt like Precious from the movie my kids and I went to see on Saturday. Seeing that movie gave me more motivation to write—to open my mouth and tell my story, paying no attention to whom I might hurt.

I was always trying to protect everyone's feelings ever since I was a child, but no one ever protected me. Even when the state got involved, you know Child Protective Services they didn't protect me. They kept sending me to more family members, who continued to abuse and harm me in ways that affect my life today.

I know my views on men and my hate toward the species that I love so much have a lot to do with what they did to me, right down to my father, who was a drug addict and did not even recognize me.

I still remember that day as if it were yesterday. I think I was about ten years old, and my mother either needed money or she was driving in

- 2 -

the area. Whatever the reason may be, we stopped at my father's crack house in the southeast part of DC.

I do not even know why she went there, because I knew he was on drugs and I was very embarrassed by the sight of him from when I saw him a couple years before.

We were sitting in my mom's gold 1990-something Toyota Camry, and my father came around the corner.

As we were sitting there, I started to observe the area.

It was full of crackheads. The house was a mess. There were many children all around the house. The woman he was living with was a crackhead, and she and my father had two of her six kids together. That made me have two little sisters, one born addicted to crack.

After seeing this sight, even though I did not have a father growing up, I was happy I did not. I believe this would have hurt me more. I could not imagine having to hide my VCR or living as my little sisters were.

All of a sudden, my father appeared at my right side window. He looked a mess.

I was thinking, *Mommy, tell me this isn't my daddy. You were joking, right? This is just another crackhead passing through, right?*

Tears were boiling inside of me, and I felt so empty inside.

"Alex, Alex," he said as he started to knock on the car window.

The thing about it is, I was sitting on the other side of my little sister, who was six years old. She started to scream like she saw a monster—well; by the looks of it he sure did look like one.

My mother intervened and said, "Alex is on the other side. You don't even know your own child."

Good, I thought. *If he does not know me, if I ever see him in the street, I won't have to claim him.*

Hold up—it is pickup time at my day care, and the parents are coming. I am so hungry. I have some black-eyed peas in the slow cooker that I bought and have not put to use till now.

My son keeps running up the steps to get ready for his grandmother's house. He calls her G'ma. Even though that woman can get under my skin, I truly appreciate her for being there for my son. She even helps from time to time with my girls, unlike my mom. It feels good to get help with one of my children's fathers and his family.

The girls' father, Marsh, who was my first ex-husband, is a sorry case. He even had the nerve to go and have another baby after twelve years two weeks ago. That made six girls for him—what a sorry excuse he is for a father.

What makes it worse is he's always around someone else's children, and he always has many little kids following behind him. I remember the times the little kids used to knock on my door and ask if Marsh could come out and play. Call me crazy, but that is strange. As soon as I was able to leave, I did.

Marsh had a lot with him. I mean, the guy was married to a fifteen-year-old girl who was also his fourth cousin, and he was twenty-three. As I look back as a grown woman, I get angry how no one cared enough to prevent all that I endured.

I used to ask myself why I suffered so much pain at such a young age. I now know that God picks certain people to live certain lives due to their strength and endurance, and I am one of those people.

It was the end of my day, and I was getting prepared to go to school. Yes, I am currently enrolled in college. I am studying criminal justice. I plan to use my degree to further my child-care business, and maybe expand my PI career.

Yes, I am a private investigator as well. That came about from an experience I had with my ex Tim; I go to court next month, hopefully on the eighteenth, to finalize that situation.

Well, that is a completely different story. We'll get to that one soon.

As I am sitting on the bottom of my steps daydreaming and waiting for my last day-care parents to arrive, the movie *Precious* pops up in my head.

Seeing that movie on Saturday saddened me, along with strengthening me. Precious had her whole present and future dictated to her, and even though I had my past dictated, I never realized how it still played a major part in my present until now.

It hurts me to know that I am still letting men hurt me. There are no harsh feelings to the few good men out there, but I am talking about the souls of the men who I now realize are also hurt.

In the area I live, there are only a few good men, and I am starting to think I need to move to another state, but I hear it is everywhere so maybe I need to move to another continent. I mean, around this area, no one has values. Women think it is normal to have baby daddies and work long hours with no father figure to help raise the children. Men think it a sport to gather up woman like they're in an auction. It is sick these days. It seems like my children will endure even worse situations unless we as people raise the upcoming generation with values. Well, don't get me preaching.

Well, it is officially one day away from my thirty-first birthday, Wednesday, November 18, 2009. After my last child left yesterday, I went to school. My son's grandmother came and got him; she even kept my middle daughter overnight. My middle daughter is practicing at Southern High School. I have no way of getting her there. My baby girl is enrolled in a performing arts school; her major is drama. That little girl has so much talent.

I just wish I had someone else to help me with my girls. Their future suffers because I am not able to participate in helping them get to practices or different events because I either have to work or money is tight.

Nevertheless, I am determined to do the best I can to allow them to flourish in their dreams.

My mom made no such attempts for me. I do remember one time I was living with my grandmother because Social Services had taken me away from my mom due to her abuse. Mrs. Mateo, my caseworker—whom I would love to meet again—sent me to a performing arts program. Mrs. Mateo knew I loved to write, and she wanted to help enhance my awareness for the arts. That exposure allowed me to appreciate the arts so much more.

I remember when we were getting ready for this big event; it was a major landmark in my life. We practiced for months; I performed ballet, tap, and modern dance. The play was a hit we had talent scouts and lots of important people there showing their support. That was my first feeling of accomplishment as a child; before then, I just thought I was bad luck.

Well, back to yesterday. Class was okay. We were talking about five-year-old Shaniya Davis, a beautiful little girl who was found dead in the rural woods about thirty miles away from her hometown after a one-week search for the little girl. Authorities said Shaniya's dad had raised the precious baby girl until last month, when he decided to let her live with her crackhead-looking mother with dreads. Accusations were that the little girl's mother offered Shaniya up for sex.

The investigation of Shaniya Davis's disappearance yielded the arrest of her mother and two men. I feel so saddened by this, and I wish—as I do for myself—that someone would have stepped up and taken control before these horrific events took place. People, we must talk for the children. Kids are innocent souls, and even when our parents do us wrong, we think that is the way of life, unless someone shows us different. Children who are abused learn the hard way. I wish I knew Shaniya personally. I would have driven all the way to Fayetteville, North Carolina, taken that baby, and raised her. She was such a beautiful little girl.

A tear falls from my eyes for Shaniya, and that tear reminds me of a poem I wrote as a hurting child at the age of ten, so in loving memory of Shaniya Davis, I dedicate my poem to you. As I look for the poem in my big box of memories. I came across so many memories and journal entries from when I was about twelve to fifteen years old expressing my feelings and emotions. I found poems that I had written in my time of pain. That was what I did best—write.

Just now, a feeling of anxiety, excitement, and relief came across me. I was saying inside that I finally found the right format to share my story. You would not imagine how many times I started to write, and each time I went through a block. Now I feel like I have the right way, and it's accelerating. Ever since I was a child, I knew my gift, and I knew one day I would write about everything I had been through. I knew it would all come out, and that time is now.

As I am writing, I want to stop and say to my inner child, "We are making it, Alex. We are on the brink of letting it all out." I feel once I finish this book, I will be able to free my inner child and let her roam. All I have done was suppress her for years, not allowing her to speak or voice her thoughts. "You are almost free," is what I tell her.

I finally found the poem. This is to you, Baby Shaniya.

Silent Tears

I go to my room and cry to myself
Tears that no one ever saw or met.
They are my silent tears, and this is their poem.
Listen to them before they are gone.
Gone to a place that's so secretive only the brain knows
where it is.

They are three little tears that mean a lot to me.
They are my silent tears, and this is their story.
Every day I cry and cry, but no one knows and that is
no lie.
I cry about three different things,
and my silent tears are going to tell you what they are
and what they mean.
Tear number one is sad and sorrow.
He cries because he hopes it is a better tomorrow,
and I cry with him. Believe me, I do I cry with him when
I am sad and blue.
Tear number two is my love tear.
He lets me know if I love or care.
This tear is closer to my heart, and I loved from the very
start.
He tells me the difference between love and hate or if a
person is just okay.
Tear number three is my self-esteem tear, and he is the
best.
When things are sad to me, he is like Superman and picks
me up and makes me happy.
He's a dear ol' tear, and I feel good when he is near.
So one day when you cry and find three little guys falling
from your eyes,
They are your silent cries, and no one else can make you
feel like your own Silent Tears.

After reading that poem again, I realize the concept now as an adult
even more than when I was a child. I said that my tears were my strength
and my comfort, but they came unnoticed to the world. I bet little Shaniya
had only her tears that were buried inside her as the only comfort she had
before she died. What sick people we have in this world. RIP Shaniya.

After school, I stopped at the carryout to get some chicken and fries.
I usually go to restaurants every day and order seafood. I have high-class
taste buds, but with the rocky economy, I just ordered some chicken.
I will save the best meal for my birthday. When I arrived home, my
daughter was taking the dogs out.

After I finished eating and taking a shower, I called my friend Robert up. He was supposed to come over here, and I told him I would call him after I left school. However, he did not answer the phone, so I tried one more time—and there he was on my other line.

Before I could realize it, he was ringing my doorbell. I like Robert a lot; I think to myself he might be the one. Once Robert walked in, we went into my room, which was located downstairs. One of my exes built this room for me last year; he thought he was going to be living here. He was surely mistaken. As Robert entered my room, I looked up at his beautiful smile, and I started to melt inside. Boy, oh boy.

Chapter 2

Happy to love
Glad to be liked
grateful to see the light
and determined not to lose sight.

Robert looks like a Mekhi Phifer-Mike Tyson mix. As the night started to become dark, Robert and I lay in the bed. While I was lying there, I prayed that the event that he and I experienced four weeks ago on his birthday did not happen again. And I prayed that he would let it go so we could move on. I know you are wondering what I am talking about. Well, if I must tell, let me get my food first. Just to give you a short description of myself, I am a short, thick lady—not fat, just right in my eyes, well, almost just right. But I still want to lose about fifteen more pounds, just to get close to the size I used to be and fit into some of those jeans in my closet, but mostly for my endurance and health.

I used to be so obsessed with my weight when I was younger. I used to vomit my food back up after I had a fatty meal. I think it was a phase I went through. As I got older, I learned the acids that came up with the vomit can ruin your teeth. I soon stopped. I paid too much for my overbite to be removed.

Well, anyway, while I was lying there beside Robert, the event of that day started to replay in my head. Robert and I had driven to Solomon's Island, Maryland, about an hour and a half away to go to this seafood restaurant on the water. It was very windy but romantic. I had just met Robert a few weeks before at this lounge about ten minutes from my house.

I was just in the process of trying to end things with my friend

Melton. Melton and I had an unhealthy relationship. It was like we both were not truly ready for each other, but we didn't want anyone else to have us either—at least that was how Melton acted. I, on the other hand, had dated and seen enough to know Melton was in my life just for the time being. Now that I sit back and think about it, I realize it was a lot of insecurities on both our parts that kept us dealing with each other; we were never meant to be more than friends.

I should have just left Melton alone the first time he tried to pop up at my house.

I remember it like it was yesterday. We had met at this nightclub. It was my first night out after getting my surgery for my tummy tuck, and I was looking good. One thing that attracts me about a man is one that is to himself, not staring down every woman. Melton seemed to be that type of guy—what a joke that was. After noticing him for an hour, I began to send him eye signals. As the club was getting close to closing, we eventually exchanged names. About two weeks later, we met up in the shopping center down the street from his house, and there we sat in my car and talked. We talked for about fifteen minutes before the phone rang. Melton answered it, and all I could hear was this woman's voice fussing and using explicit language. He tried to smile out of embarrassment. But it was too late; I had already heard everything. He then stated that it was his youngest son's mom and he had to leave to get him ready to go home. I said okay, so we hugged, and we both said we would talk to each other soon.

I should have known from the sound of his son's mother's voice that Melton had some stuff with him. As the days turned into nights and the weeks passed, Melton and I became closer friends. But all that soon changed when I realized he was cheap and spoiled. I think by him being a light-skinned, pretty boy, he was used to women catering to him. Well, I was determined not to be one of those women. After a couple months went past with no real commitment and no real anything, I decided to stop the relationship.

I started to date a new guy a couple weeks later, and once Melton realized I was no longer calling him, he popped up at my house. It was the daytime and I was very upset. We began to argue and I sent him on his way, but we later became friends again. But I still didn't expect for him to pop up while Robert and I were dating. By the time I met Robert, Melton and I were cool, but we were again drifting away from our friendship.

As I sit here and think and reflect, I start to drift back a couple years prior to the time I decided to leave Marsh, my ex-husband, after six years of pure hell. I think of all the many immature tactics he pulled because I left him. One incident that stands out the most was him throwing nails in the street because he was worried about me having company. He had nothing on me. I had just purchased my first house at the age of twenty-one all by myself. Marsh was so jealous of me growing up he refused to help me with the process of purchasing a new home. So I went and bought it all alone. This was better for me. At twenty-one, after being locked in a cave from the age of fifteen, I was finally feeling free, and I took full advantage of the resources life had to offer. At that time, nothing was more important to me than my God and my children. I was finally gaining dignity and independence.

After purchasing my first home, I had the strength to end things with Marsh. He was so devastated by me ending the relationship, he started to act very scary. I had watched enough Lifetime stories to know where this could lead to if I went back. One day right after we were giving each other a so-called break, Marsh drove around my house and saw a car that he never noticed before. Marsh called me on the phone screaming and yelling, saying he was going to flatten the tires on this car if I had someone in my house. I can remember sitting on my couch, upset and fussing with Marsh. The fact was I did have company, but who was he to tell me what to do? We were not together anymore, and he already had a seventeen-year-old Hispanic girl living in the apartment with him, claiming he was just helping her out.

Once I found this out, I started to realize that I was never special to him. I was just another victim. I knew Marsh was sleeping with the girl because he had a tendency to sleep with young needy girls—just like I once was. It later came out. I sometimes wonder about the young girl who had a new baby by him. She was only twenty-three, and he was thirty-eight. Well, at least he kept it in the over-eighteen range this time, but I wonder if Marsh had her do all the things he wanted me to do.

By the time my company left my house to go home, two hours had passed, and I knew Marsh had done just what he said. I didn't tell the guy what threats Marsh had made about his car.

As we approached the car, I couldn't help but look to see if Marsh had actually followed through on his threats. Not to my surprise, he did:

the guy's tire was flat. Marsh had sliced the tire. Once the guy saw this, he became very upset and disoriented, and he then realized the guy I was arguing with on the phone had done this to his tire. I was so pissed because I now had to pay out of my pocket for the guy's car to get towed home and then replace the tire. So you can see why I feared men popping up after I let them go.

As I matured, I started to realize that some men like controlling women so much that they don't know how to act when a woman controls them effortlessly.

Chapter 3

In the world where there is so much pain, if you close your eyes for two seconds, you will experience peace. In life we have to close our eyes to the negatives to receive the full experience of happiness.

Today is Friday, November 20, 2009, and my birthday was yesterday. I enjoyed my birthday but was very disappointed by some of the main people who say they care—but then the one who I least expected to call me, Melton, did. I was at a loss for words. I have lost a lot of respect for Robert. He texted me at 4:45 a.m. on his way to work on my birthday, but not once did he call me all day. And get this—he even had the nerve to call me this morning and ask how my night went. I wanted to say, "What do you mean how my night went? You didn't even call." But I just said great and then got off the phone As I think about it, Robert and I are still getting to know each other, so it's too early for me to set expectations. But a phone call on the day of my birthday would have been nice.

The one thing I gained from my life experience was self-pride and never to let them (outsiders) get the best of me. As I sit here hurt inside, I fade away to a place where I once was a child, where I cared about someone and he made me feel like I had to please him. I start to think back to my grandmother's common-law husband, E. T. I was living with my grandmother at the time in the Northeast part of DC. I was in the sixth grade, about eleven or twelve. My mother called my grandmother to pick me up because I changed the grades on my report card so badly that you could not even see the grade when I was done. Instead of my mother getting in trouble once again from the state for beating on me, she called my grandmother. I was so happy to live with my grandmother;

she understood me better than my mother ever did. Once I moved in with my grandmother, she was granted temporary custody of me for the second time.

Living with my grandmother was a little piece of heaven. I didn't have to worry about any utilities getting disconnected or my mother flipping out on me for nothing. But all of that soon changed. My grandmother's common-law husband, E. T., was the creepiest old man on earth to me. It was not his appearance; it was the things he tried to make me do to him. I hated him. He knew I was abused at home, but he didn't care. He turned around and tried to abuse and use me for his own sexual pleasures. He abused me in a totally different way from what I was used to. He tried to harm me sexually. I hated him for it. It was disgusting the many gestures he made to me while my grandmother was at work or out of the room. He would come in the house and try to bribe me with treats and money to touch him.

The vague memories of E. T. coming in the house, pulling out nasty books, showing them to me, and making me watch them with him while he had me do acts only a grown-up should do were unbearable. I wish I'd had the guts to say to him, "Leave me alone. I hate you." I remember the time I did stand up to him and said, "No, I do not want to participate in your acts of sexual molestation." Will I didn't use those exact words. But I refuse to participate any longer. That was when living with my grandmother became a nightmare. He would come in the house, walk right past me, and say nothing—as if I were not there. *I'd rather not talk to you either*, I thought. It was better that way instead of him constantly trying to exploit my body.

What was it about my body, I used to wonder, that would make a grown man excited? I mean, at the time I had no breasts and no real curves. I just could not figure it out, so I started to think it was normal for some men to touch little girls. I realized they had a problem, but maybe they sensed some little girls understood their sickness. And I was one of them. The more I rejected him, the meaner he started to be. He even would buy candy, chips, and cakes—all the things he didn't eat and knew I loved—and set them on the dining room table, daring me to touch or ask him for some. It was manipulation at its best. He was saying to me if I wanted those things, I must do what he wanted.

My grandmother noticed the behavior. She once asked why we

were not talking, and he answered, "Alex knows why." I wanted to say, "Because he wants to molest me and have me do things I am not supposed to do until I am married," but I loved my grandmother too much and I knew she loved this pervert. Besides, I wondered if she would believe me, especially after I had recently told her about my mother's boyfriend and what he tried to do.

I started thinking she would be like, "This little girl always got something with her." On top of that, I was having problems at home. I just decided to keep my mouth shut.

I remember one time while I was still living with my grandmother, I got so excited because I found out E. T. was finally going to leave and I could finally be happy again living with my grandmother alone. I was sitting in my grandmother's living room when she called out to me to get my shoes on and get in the car. At that time I was watching my favorite movie "Roll of Thunder, Hear My Cry" and didn't want to move. But as soon as I heard my grandmother's keys dangle, I jumped up. And off we went, riding down the city streets. Before I knew it, we were on the strip where E. T. hung out at night with his buddies.

I asked Grandma what we were doing around there. "We going to catch him," she replied. My eyes popped from the tone of voice and look on my grandmother's face. I had never seen her so mad. Grandma was usually a very mild-mannered woman. I began to get sad; seeing my grandmother like this was not a good feeling. Then suddenly the car sped off, and my grandmother was driving fast. Before I knew it, Grandma was chasing the car in front of us. And I was in a moment of disbelief. What was going on? Hold up, it was E. T. driving in front of us, and he had a lady in the passenger seat. E. T. turned the corner, and my grandmother turned behind him. He must have realized it was my grandmother because he sped faster and we were on a wild-goose chase. Eventually we lost him.

As we turned our vehicle the opposite way and began to head home. I looked up at my grandmother again. This time I saw tears flooding her eyes. I looked down, trying to focus my emotions somewhere else. Once we arrived back at her apartment, she sent me to bed and started to pack his belongings. I rushed to bed, waiting for the next day when E. T, and all his belongings were going to be gone. But my little excitement turned the opposite when I woke up and he was still there, cooking breakfast and singing. I looked at my grandmother, but she would not give me eye contact, and from there on, I never asked any questions. As time passed, later in my adult years, E. T. finally departed due to her finding out she had breast cancer.

I saw E. T. with the same lady again while I was working in the mall. But this time they had a little girl with them. "Daddy, Daddy," the little girl called out while looking at E. T. *Wow*, I thought. He had what looked to me to be a seven-year-old daughter and he was at least sixty years old. I then became saddened because I knew that innocent little girl was probably being molested by her own father, just like he once molested me. I began to shake my head and hid in the crowd, hoping he would not notice me. I just wish I knew back then what I know now.

I later found out he did this same thing to my younger aunt. She didn't tell me until I was in my mid-twenties. I was at her house visiting, and we sat at the table eating crabs as she allowed the skeletons of our family to pierce my ears. She told me why she was so attracted to old men and how alcohol was introduced to her and why she became a drunk. And everything all started from him. My aunt shared with me how he would bribe her too with goods. She even told me about how he turned her on to liquor and got her drunk and raped her while my grandmother was at work. To make matters worse, he was her first sex partner at thirteen years old. My aunt held my hand and confided in me with all her deepest, darkest secrets. She stated how my grandmother didn't believe her when she tried to tell.

After sitting there reflecting on all she endured, I found myself getting madder and madder by the moment. How did my grandmother ever feel comfortable leaving me with him? All this time, I was protecting her by keeping the secret from her. And all the time, I was the one needing protection. I remember once I sat down and talked to a group of older people, and someone made a comment that families used to think it was normal for molestation and rape to go on among family members. The group was doing research to find out the source of molestation. As I sat there listening to everyone, I started to think maybe that was how my family thought. I wondered. But I am here to say it is not normal, and it's not okay. Every time someone you love or look up to abuses you in any way, you lose your sense of pride and innocence; you lose yourself.

Chapter 4

Love is not always the gain of another person's heart, but it sometimes comes in life's pain with a lesson where the pain is the rebirth of your soul, and just then is when you can receive love.

As I sit here trying to get my mind-set clear, I let out a small sigh of how funny the mind really works. And of how even when you try to be nothing like the way you were raised, your mind can detect unhealthy relationships as representations of love and you would not even know the difference.

Today is Thursday, December 10, 2009. Thanksgiving was okay. Not much has been going on; I've just been working. The day after Thanksgiving, I finally heard from Robert. We ended up going to the Cheesecake Factory, which was where we went on our first date. We talked about everything, and I expressed myself to him about how his behavior had been making me feel. Once we got over that hurdle, Robert and I have been hanging strong. I will not talk too fast; Robert and I just got back from a short weekend trip. It was very relaxing. Robert and I click so well, and unlike other men, Robert is more sincere than what I have been attracting lately. Robert's mom and my grandmother even hit it off. Last Saturday they went to Atlantic City with each other. It was cute seeing two senior citizens hang out like girlfriends; the older by ten years, which was my grandmother, pushed the younger in a wheelchair.

These last few days, I have been doing a lot of soul-searching, trying to make small changes in my life that will lead to big changes. Besides hanging with Robert occasionally, I have not really been interested in rushing into love at this point. I have just been sitting back and seeing where God will lead. I can say I do have true feelings for Robert and I love his company; except for his beliefs on the United States government, we are like two peas in a pod. It's not that I don't believe in what he talks about; I just want him to do more research and tell me how he can actually change the way we live in this slavery-written world.

I now realize that sometimes people win by not even fighting, but by walking away. It is December 15, 2009. I have been practicing this, but it just seems that lately I forgot how to do it. Not every battle is worth fighting for, and the real loser is the one not aware of that.

I almost died without finishing my book. I feel real dumb. I just want to smack myself. I wonder how I could be as dumb as to make the choice I made last night.

The night started out well. I had fasted for three days, and was looking real good and feeling fine. My dress fit me perfectly; it hit every angle. I never knew a body could look so delicious. I mean I looked so good I was full over the sight of myself. But soon all the good feeling went away fast when I awoke the next morning not even realizing how I got where I was and not even remembering hitting the pole. It all was a vague memory. All I know is the valet gave me my keys. I started driving my car everything from there seems like a dream. In my dream I drove on the island, and swept the pole. So when I found out it was more than a dream I became confused. I don't remember anything.

"Good morning," a voice said to me. "Do you know you were real drunk last night?"

"Huh?" I replied as I strained my eyes to see the person clearly.

"Girl, look at your car. It is ruined on the driver's side."

"What!" I said with a disfigured look of confusion on my face. I quickly got up and ran to the bathroom.

There in the bathroom, I started to feel very light-headed and drifted away in yet another memory. Before I could realize it, I was standing in the middle of my mom's boyfriend's shop. "Leave me alone," I cried out. "You are supposed to be taking me to get my sister. Why are we here with no one?"

I looked up, and I was a nine-year-old child again, talking to my mother's boyfriend. He had sidetracked from picking me up from school; we were supposed to get my little sister afterward and then go to his home until my mom got off work, but we ended up at his job. He owned a barbershop, and there would be no one there but him and me. As I stood outside the shop, I started to become frightened. My heart started to pound. The fear of what this man could do to me was so unbearable it was frightening. He had the look of evil upon his face as he looked at me and smiled and said, "What's wrong?"

My silent tears started to pour down my face, and I turned cold emotionally. I shut my body down to block out anything that he tried to do to me. It was like my mind had gone to another place and I could not feel. I basically took my soul from my body and placed it on the side. On numerous occasions he had tried to molest me, but he never had me all to himself so he could never go but so far, my sister would always be around which limited the sexual abuse he could do to me. Now I would be all alone with him.

I remember standing there wondering why my mom allowed me to be with a man like him. I started to shake in fear of what he was going to do to me. I was not ready for my innocence to be robbed from me. I mean, why didn't my mother have a feeling of what he was capable of? She always used to ask me if he did something to me, but I never felt comfortable enough to tell. I know now as a mom myself, if I felt the need to ask my child if my man did something to her, he is not the man for me. I guess he seemed to make her happy. I remember she used to always say she would kill anyone who ever did something to me. Then who would take care of me if she were in jail? My father was a crackhead. The thought of losing the only parent I had, whether she was good or not, was way too much pressure on a young child, so I said nothing. But if I even had a notion someone was capable of abusing my child in any way, I would not allow my child to be around him. I certainly wouldn't date him. Why didn't my mom think of things that way?

As we walked in the shop, I started to look around. The setup was nice. The walls were freshly painted, and the interior designs were appealing. "Come here, Alex," he yelled out to me. I walked in the front room, and he began to molest me. Why did everyone see me as a weak person that they could just take advantage of? Was I put on this earth to be abused and broken by everyone that was supposed to care?

Before you knew it, I was lying on the floor, and he had pulled my pants down. "Just be patient. I will not hurt you," he whispered.

I was too scared to say what I was thinking. "Leave me alone, you pervert. Why are you trying to steal my innocence when you have my mother?"

Before anything else could happen, just as he attempted to open the eyes of a child, the phone rang. What a relief, I sighed. Thank you, God. I jumped up, and my silent tears started to rush down from my eyes like a leaky water faucet once again.

As I sat on the toilet in the bathroom dazed, an irritated a knock brought me back to reality. "You okay?" the voice said. "Go look at your car. You tore it up."

I did not want to hear that. I just got my car out of the shop from my sister's fender bender, and now my beautiful white Mercedes-Benz was again going to have to get worked on.

Now that the reality of my accident has truly kicked in, I am sitting under the dryer at home, and it is Thursday, December 17, 2009. Yesterday, Robert and I did a little shopping. I ran into Quiznos and quickly parked in a handicapped parking space, and now today a friend pointed out to me I have a $200.00 parking ticket. Damn! It just seems like I need to really get back grounded with the Lord because my luck is really testing me. I spoke to Melton and found out he is making things work with his ex, Natalie. I guess she's footing the bill and the relationship. Better her than me. I need a real man, and to tell you the truth, I am not sure what direction Robert and I are going, but he seems like a better fit for me than Melton.

As I sat on my couch on Friday, December 18, 2009, I started to daydream, asking myself why I cared for Melton and others like him. I finally came up with the answer. They were the spitting image of my past and of all the men who hurt me. They all were charming, sick, and very deceitful. They were so deceitful you didn't even know that you were being deceived. The catch with Melton, he always made it seem like he was unaware of his own ways. Whatever happened to him in his childhood really messed him up. I remember the day we called our self-bonding, when he shared his secret with me. I told him about me getting married young, and he told me about being molested as a child. I used to wonder during our relationship if that was why he had intimacy issues with women. He even told me the only woman he ever let get close to him cheated on him, and he told me of the damage it caused after she left. I think that is why I let Melton get close to me—because I felt sorry for him. That was the same reason why I let the people who hurt me in the past get away with it.

For some ridiculous reason, I felt sorry for them, but who is going to feel sorry for me? I am learning that I have to love myself or I will continue to repeat the same things. I am so tired of feeling sorry.

Chapter 5

As I look up at the sky, I can see the birds flying above my head, and the telephone lines are going at an angle. The peace I experience from being outside is remarkable. It's like the atmosphere of nature allows my inner soul to come out and my words to flow on paper, like a ballerina on her tippy toes doing a plié, so delicate and soft.

Today is March 19, 2010. It's been awhile since I wrote last, and a lot has been going on. Robert and I have been hanging in there for going on six months. I ran into this guy named Quincy, but that was nothing. He appeared right at the time Robert and I were starting to go through a rocky patch, but nothing came of it. That was because I want to do right by my relationship, at least while there is still a commitment, because karma is crazy, and besides, Quincy reminded me too much of my past.

Robert and I had a major bump in our relationship this weekend. His ex came to town from California, and he ignored my phone call and even turned the phone off. I was so hurt and ready to move on. After talking to my sister and her reminding me that he was a good guy, I just stepped back because I do know there are different stages in a relationship and Robert and I are still in the beginning stage. So I took the incident like Robert and his ex had history that they needed to clear out. Besides, he needed to be around her to realize that he did not want her anymore. I will at least try to give him the benefit of the doubt.

Melton and I were still letting our separate paths go along as well. But my guard is still up. Life has changed so much, and so has my outlook on relationships. I once looked at Robert and me as fantasy, but now I see fantasy is only on television; this is reality. Relationships go through their share of trials and tribulations and stages of letting go of their past. I hope this doesn't drag on long because my patience for love at this point is very thin.

I can say I am starting to realize more and more that I need to live my life to my fitting, not for what makes others happy. I will not neglect myself to please anyone or fit into a fantasy. If someone loves me, he will love me and accept me for who God created me to be, not what he is trying to form me into. I have taken on a take-care-of-me-or-leave-me attitude in my life.

The situation I had with Robert over the weekend certainly hurt me. I sat back, looked at myself and my past and said, "I have been through this one time too many. I am so over this." So I said to myself, "Alexandria, you have to let go and let God. Everything must happen naturally and not by my fear. So I now release the pain of fear and self-doubt and replace it with courage and self-love."

Regardless of the things a person is trying to prevent, when it comes to someone else, there is not much you can do but pray and let it alone. Trying to control anything but yourself is a waste of energy; the only thing we can control in life is ourself. Once a person allows herself to develop and grow, that's when she's able to acknowledge and receive the gifts God has in store for her.

Even as a young child, I always had a relationship with God. I used to wonder how I loved and grew so much respect for a being I had little knowledge about. I was not raised going to church on a regular basis. My mother and other family members took me to their church, but I never really knew what the preacher was saying. I kind of zoned out in church, just like I did in school. But I always had this love for God bestowed within my soul, and as I went through life, the vessel in my heart grew more and more for this being I had no real clue about. As I got in my preteens, I would read the Bible to learn more, and I also watched my Grandma J and the way she respected God. She honored the Sabbath day and kept it holy by not working, and she would read me Bible stories at bedtime. With her love and dedication and this connection that I felt, I knew that God was the key to all my misery and this world was just a preparation for the man above, so I tried to live my days in hopes of being honored enough to get there.

Today is April 15, 2010, almost a month later, and my relationship with Robert is over. As of last Sunday, I decided to put myself first and stop the self-destruction of my crumbling heart. I can't believe the thought of not wanting to be here came over me on Sunday night. Yes I had thoughts of death. I didn't feel this way because of Robert but mainly because I have not allowed myself to heal from all the other failed relationships and past pains. I can't believe I, Mrs. Move On, Next, Whatever, had gotten to the point where hope was lost. As I stood there reflecting back on my life, I decided that no one and no situation was worth it and that the biggest payback was to succeed against all odds.

So that's what I will continue to do. Wow, I am finally closing the chapter between Robert and me. What a surprise! It came totally unexpected, but life is unexpected. After his behavior and his pulling back, it was totally needed. The last couple of weeks were very disturbing right up to Sunday. This guy had the nerve to tell me he loved me but was scared of the responsibility of family and was not ready. *What did you think you were getting into?* I thought to myself. *With the type of woman I am, you should have known you were liable to get caught up. Well, anyway, I see you are a young boy, and I should have just seen you for what it was—fun. But know I started to allow myself to dream, dreams that were too big for you to fulfill.*

I knew once I wrote my letter, that was going to be the deal breaker. So on Monday morning, I decided to e-mail him—five days before the actual breakup. The letter read:

> Robert,
>
> First, let me start off by saying I really enjoyed you in my life, but like the weather changes, so has our relationship. I am glad to be writing this to you instead of saying it because when two people talk, the words are not always being listened to. I know you said you don't have time for emotions, but the world is just one big emotion, good or bad. In life we feel them every day, all day. It's something you cannot get away from. I see you are going through a lot of changes and you are totally pulling back from me. I would be a fool with my head stuck in my ass if I didn't acknowledge what is being

dealt to me. I am truly shocked and surprised because I thought we were better than this.

I meant my text when I said you are a good boyfriend and I trust you, but you have changed as well from how you once treated me. I have no real clue why you are acting this way. This is usually a sign of a third person coming in. I hope that is not the case, but for what other real reason would a man pull back from a woman he loves and wants to be with? *Please tell me*.

I have exhausted all my energy trying to get your attention and actually belittled myself by popping up, crying, and leaving a voice message, all in the attempt of trying to save what we once had. I truly care for you, but I know love is not supposed to feel like this. I have no real clue why you are acting this way, but I am hurting myself more by holding on. So badly I wanted us to work, and I saw myself really fight for a relationship that I thought was worth fighting for. You are not an easy person to get along with and you know this, and you know how you been treating me is not right. I am a real person with feelings, and we both promised not to hurt each other. I guess in some cases, we will always see differently on relationships and mutual respect. All of a sudden you started pulling back and saying you were not going to do the most important thing to make a relationship work (communication). So I have come to the realization that things may never go back to what I was holding onto.

I used to look at you as my knight. Now I am left confused. If for any reason I made you feel smothered, I was just loving you and wanting to be with you. I loved the chemistry we had with each other and tomorrow is not guaranteed, so I wanted to feel the moment whenever I could. I never wanted to take up all your time. I just was trying to establish grounds of love and trust, and the only way to do that is to spend time, so when we are apart, we both know our love for each other is enough to withstand all other distractions that will play a part in trying to pull us apart. I have decided to give you what you want, and that is freedom. Just remember the grass is not always greener on the other side. And just like age, everything gets old, and what's more important is having that special person to grow old with. I know you have goals and are trying to establish yourself. I was willing to be that rock beside you and help you along the way in any way I could. All I needed from you was security. And we could have done the damn thing.

"Love is having that one person who would not leave you for another person, job, or their own selfishness. Real love is when you stop thinking of yourself and think of someone else's happiness, and by doing that you are happy." I hope that one day you will understand what I mean.

Love always, Alex

Again I was finding myself bending over backward, trying to make things work. Now I was fed up. Listening to my sister, I thought to myself, *I should have left him after the ex-girlfriend thing. And to think Ocean City helped.*

It patched things up short-term, but after Sunday and him bringing my kids in the middle, I started to reflect on whom it was I was really dating and the way he was able to carry me for his ex. I then started to realize this man was not a branch, but just a leaf passing by. So on Sunday I decided to put him in my recycle bin, and today I will empty it out.

It is crazy how a person I once loved changed into someone I'm not attracted to. I am talking about Melton. For the past couple weeks, we have been cool, both talking to each other like friends about our situations. I am so glad that there is nothing there. He came past during my lunch, and we talked and ate. I made a joke that if Robert stopped by, he would be the one in the house for a change. We both laughed.

Today is Thursday, April 22, 2010. I am still struggling to get over the situation. Robert came past on Friday, and we talked for two hours. It just seemed so odd. I wanted to shake him and say, "Why are you doing me like this?" Well, now as I think, I am starting to feel that his ex has a lot to do with this, and I wonder if he had sex with her when she was here. Maybe she is pregnant or something; I do not know, but it's got to be something.

I sent him a closure letter yesterday. I knew in order for me to totally shake him, I had to do what I do best, and that's write. It read:

> This will be short. I am very hurt about the way you have been treating me. You really tried to hit me below the belt when you blamed your behavior on my having children. I just started realizing it's not my kids, it's you. You are not ready nor mature enough to be a good role model for my children; that's all you would have had to be. The worst thing you could have ever done was blame your behavior on my children. They are my world, and they mean more to me than any relationship. I am ready to let this situation go emotionally because I have rage in my heart for how you tried to make me seem alienated by being a mother of three wonderful, attractive kids.
>
> I realize I and my children deserve so much better. You were not the only one choosing. I guess I was in love with a fake image all this time. I thought you were real and sincere about your actions. Remember Christmas and going shopping, spending time dancing and rapping with us? Dinner around the table, skating, movies with the kids —I guess all that was just you trying to get in my underwear. Wow. I never knew you could be so evil until now.
>
> Like you, I want to move on and pray God give me the strength. I know I will have no problem getting someone to step up and be that man in my life. I just hope you have success in your endeavors, because God has a way of getting you back when you treat good people wrong. *I know that until you do right, everything you do will fail.* I do want to say I pray each day to be able to forgive you for all the pain you caused on my side, and I want to thank you for allowing me to really see what I was falling in love with.

I hoped if he had any real emotions, my letter affected him. But it seems as if he is emotionally inept. I am so ready to move on and be happy, single, and free.

Today is April 26, 2010. I spent over $600.00 talking to a counselor. I never liked talking to anyone about my problems, but I felt so empty and devastated that I needed to lean on someone, so I found a relationship counselor and made an appointment. During our talk, the counselor guided me in areas I already knew I needed to address, but I had buried them deep within.

Why? is the question I ask. Why have I become so codependent on relationships and now I feel like I am some kind of addict waiting for my next hit? I am going through withdrawal or something, but I am starting to realize it is far from worth it.

I definitely need to cleanse my aura and meditate. I need to start over like new and leave the past where it is. But for some odd reason, there is a purpose our path met and a lesson we both must learn, and I am determined to find out what that lesson is.

I wish sometimes I was still green to the world, untouched emotionally. Then I would see things with less emotion, but then I guess if I did, then I would not be able to notice the present that the Lord is preparing for me. So on that note, I say, Robert, I dedicate LeToya Luckett's song "Not Anymore" to you. And I write my own version of it:

> And on this day, I refuse to give you any more energy over my life, and I rebuke Satan in the name of Jesus Christ. What the devil wishes for bad, I ask the Lord to turn into good. Whoosh, I can't wait until I finish this book and success is staring at me like the brightest star shining over the universe. As I stand right by that star, I will look down on all the vultures and vampires who have been trying to steal my blood, and there I will finally shine the very light that kills them with a smile. And then I will truly find peace.

Robert, as I end this chapter in my book, I want you to know the chapter is also ended in my heart. Like I said to you when I called you on Saturday and you were going out of town, "I truly appreciate your presence in my life, and I learned that what I thought I wanted was not what I needed. Through this pain I have gained a lot. I wish the best for you and the better for me. As I type these last words, the chapter of you is closed."

I am starting to realize that until I deal with my past, I am not truly ready for my future.

I guess all the people in my life that write me off as just another female will one day see I am very different.

Chapter 6

I am a real solider. I will fight for what I believe in, go to war for what is right, keep my head up with pride and dignity, and I will not go down until God says it is all right.

Today is May 26.2010, one month since my last entry, this weekend felt weird for me. I went on a couple dates and one speed date with this guy at Panera Bread. What a weird but understanding date. The start of the date was very different the guy started saying he was tired of going on dates and paying for women he either did not like or that he would never see again. As I sat there listening to him ramble I looked at my watch planning my escape route, I was glad he did not waste any money on me as well because with that approach. I was not going to call him either. I still was not ready for a relationship, but going out on dates and socializing helps me not sit at home and think about Robert.

Talk about going on dates, I had this one date on Saturday with Greg. Greg is a thirty-nine-year-old man who is a navy recruiter. Greg was not from the area, and our date went pretty smooth. Well, that was until at the end he told me I was the most expensive date he ever had. I know the meal was $115.00, but damn, if that is a lot, what are you used to—drive-throughs? After that statement I silently thought to myself, *Robert, what did you get me into?*

Today is May 28, 2010. I am sitting on my bed talking to William. William is a cool guy. But yet again, he too has closeness issues; I know there is no substance to our developing friendship. But he works for right now. With my experience, I am able to read a person in two minutes. I guess that's why I didn't ever allow my heart to get too attached. But then I met Robert.

Today is Wednesday, June 02, 2010. I went to the Christian bookstore and bought a prayer journal and a self-help book. I know God is trying to reach out to me, and after writing in my prayer journal, I am determined to not call on a maintenance man for any plumbing jobs, but try my best to turn to God because I know he can clear all my clogs.

I now realize that when I tried to go get baptized in September 2009 and the guest speaker went overtime, I knew then until God felt I was really ready to denounce all the things of the flesh, I was not ready, so I am on my path to try yet again to denounce them. As I sit in my kitchen typing on my computer on this windy yet beautiful spring day, I can hear the sound of my 120-pound Akita mix barking at another stranger walking past.

Drifting away into another memory, I start to dig deep within myself and come up with a time when I was about ten years old, in the fifth grade. I was getting ready for school, and my mother checked my book bag to make sure I was not sneaking anything to school. As she looked in my bag, I remember feeling scared, and anxiety started to rush my body. I had some fake nails in a bag. and I knew if she found them, she was going to go off. I had not opened the bag of nails or even put them on; I did not have any glue. One of the girls from school got them for me after I gave her a dollar that I received from Grandma J. I love Grandma J; she was my savior. She and my godmother Belinda were the main people in my life who showed me love. And when my mom treated me wrong or could not afford to buy me clothes or shoes, they were there.

I remember a time I was in the fourth grade and Mom was treating me bad. I had fifty cents in my pocket, and I had it all planned out. Right after school I usually would wait outside for my after-school van to come and pick me up, so as soon as school let out, I ran out the side of the building. I ran fast until I was out of sight and mind. It was a good thing that the bus was coming. Back then, tokens showed up in the machine as worth twenty-five cents; I learned that from catching the bus with Grandma J's daughter. Livie and I spent a lot of time together; she was a great aunt to me. I want to visit her now, but it hurts me to see her in the condition she is in. You see, Livie has cerebral palsy, and as the years go on, it gets worse. I hear she can't move, but she still is in school and trying to work. That lady has the determination of a strongly built wall that refuses to fall. I love you, Livie.

Hold up; I am calling Grandma J. It's been a year since I last spoke to her. The phone is ringing. Wow, Grandma still has the old voice-mail machine. Well, there is no answer; maybe I will try later. Back to the story.

I nicely put my quarter in the bus and received my flash pass. I had just sat down when it was time for me to transfer buses. When I arrived at my destination, I bought a bag of chips and got on the next bus. Before you knew it, I was at Grandma J's house. Once Grandma saw my little face at the door, she could do nothing but smile and offer to let me come in. Grandma once told me about when I was small and she was reading me a story, I looked up to her and said, "Grandma, I don't want to die."

"Why, Alex?" she asked.

"Because I want to be with you," I responded. She said she laughed as if I thought she were not going to heaven. I love that lady.

I asked Grandma J if I could call 411 to get the number of the day care to let the director know I was okay and to let my mother know I was fine and not to worry. I begged Grandma J not to let her know I was there. I just wanted a happy day or night where someone showed me love and hugged me, and I knew I was going to get it at Grandma J's house. Grandma J did not want to lie; she was a churchgoing woman, and I sometimes went to church with her—that was if I did not mind being in church on Saturdays. I actually liked going to her church and even had a friend named Tasha.

Tasha was a lot of trouble, I remember. I thought this boy at church was cute. Tasha went straight to him and told him I liked him, and then she lied and said I was thirteen. He was like fifteen, and I was really eleven. When he came over to me while we stood at line for an after-church dinner, he started to talk. He asked me my name and age, and I yelled out, "Alex, eleven!" When he heard the age eleven, he flipped. I had no clue that he was fifteen and that Tasha had lied about my age. After that incident, I was too embarrassed to ever want to go back to that church. One time, Grandma J let me spend the night over at Tasha's grandma's house, because they were good church buddies and this girl was trying to invite boys over once her grandma went to sleep. I was like, "This girl is wild." Tasha's grandma's house was scary, but the one thing

I loved about her grandma's house was that it was huge; she had a three-level row home with a whole lot of rooms. As time went on, Grandma J banned me from hanging with Tasha.

Later on in my teens, there was a time when I was with Marsh—I think I was seventeen—and Tasha and I got back in touch with each other. She was running wild, and I let her stay a couple of weeks at my place. I was scared to let any woman stay there because the last time we let family stay with us, I had a feeling something was not right. Marsh and I had just come back from the country from the funeral for his distant aunt, whom he never met. While there, we met some of his family members on his father's side. The one cousin that stood out—rest in peace, she is now dead—was his cousin Amy. Marsh and Amy exchanged names, and I instantly became appalled. I know, you're probably saying, "Why? That's his cousin." But so was I.

Two months passed, and Amy and her daughter came to visit us for a month. Things were fine at first, until I started seeing Marsh do a lot of suspicious things. I remember coming home and finding him peeking at Amy while she took a bath. He tried to convince me it was nothing, but a few days later, I went off and Amy left. I just kept praying for the day I too could walk out the door. Once Tasha came, I kept her in my full sight, but she was not interested in Marsh. She started to act crazy and jealous, wanting to be with me intimately. I had to let her go fast. Last I heard, she was on drugs and had had two little boys.

Grandma allowed me to stay, and when my mother sent my other grandmother's common-law husband, the pervert E. T. over, Grandma J told him I was not there. Later that night, we called my mom and told her, and they agreed to let me spend the night.

As I was standing there scared, my mother reached in the bag and pulled out the nails. She quickly looked at me and with disappointment she started to beat me yet again. This lady beat me so bad I had bruises on every part of my body. I was so hurt that when I went to school, I could not even sit down. Usually when my mom bruised or hurt me, I would defend her, but as I sat in a dazed state of mind at my desk, my teacher noticed I was not like myself and sent me to the office. As soon as I arrived, they knew my situation. You see, I was in the system as an abused child, and if the school noticed, they were to call Social Services immediately. And on this day, they sure did.

I just wished my mom had stopped after the first incident. It all started at the age of seven, and all I could remember was rolling on the living room floor and going to school with a left black eye. At this time, I thought it was normal for parents to blacken their child's eye if the child made them mad. When I arrived at school all happy with my legs swinging as I sat at my desk, my teacher, Mrs. Craig, sent me to the office, As I was sitting in the office, the school counselor started asking me questions about my eye. I just simply said, "My Mommy did it," without even realizing that I had just opened up a can of worms and the beginning of the court systems regulating my life and household. Well, not really; my mom's girlfriend did that for her a year later.

The counselor was astonished by what I shared with her. I just looked at her like, "What's wrong?" As I was sitting there playing with my fingers, a police officer came walking in. The police officer escorted me home, once I arrived, all I remember was my mother looking at me like I did something wrong.

As I stood at the top of the steps, all I remember hearing was the police officer warning my mother that if an incident like this ever happened again, I was going to be taken away. As the policeman was leaving out the door, he smiled up at me.

Not even a year went by before the next incident of abuse happened. At that age, I started to write. I remember being in my social worker's office and writing my first children's book. I would write to allow myself to focus on a fantasy world where I had control. My social worker saw my skills and encouraged me to keep it up. It is now my first book to get published.

Oh, my goodness. Today is June 20, 2010. Robert and I hung out last night; he called me earlier that day saying he missed me. I was on my road to recovery. They say it takes twenty-one days to break a habit, so I will start over.

Today is July1, 2010, and it is ten o'clock in the morning. I have homework to do and an invitation to Ocean City with this guy who says he likes me and he's been showing it. I can tell he is a good guy, but I am not sure I am ready to receive that right now. Last night I had a date, but he was running late so I canceled—plus it seemed like he was preoccupied, you know, telling me he's thirty minutes away and then when thirty minutes have passed, he calls and says he'll be here in thirty to forty minutes.

Well, a new day, and now it is, August 07, 2010. I have a lot to update you on. After listening to Joyce Meyers every morning and praying for God to help me heal, I decided to block everyone's numbers from my cell phone and home. It feels great. It has been four days now, and they have no way of contacting me unless they pop up at my house. I can truly say I feel good and am 89 percent over Robert. A lot has been going on besides that. On Tuesday, I had a date to hang out, but I was not in the mood to, so I decided to go see the male strippers.

After leaving, I decided to go to the Neighbor Restaurant. It's always fast-paced at night. They have karaoke, a DJ, and lots of good guys. But I was not going for them anyway. I was hungry, and watching the atmosphere was very entertaining. Once I arrived, I saw my cousin and some of his friends, along with some of my fans, in other words, people who want to know more about me. Then I saw *him*. No, not Robert. This guy's name is Paul. Paul was a guy I would run into from time to time, but we never really said much besides hello; we would just give each other a stare. Well, as I was sitting at the bar ordering my food, Paul came up beside me. We exchanged numbers, and he has started to call me every day. I'm just not feeling Paul as I'm sitting on my bed.

With the conversation with Melton ringing in my head, I wrote a statement on my Facebook that triggered a reaction in him. I simply stated, "It's funny someone you once thought was attractive, once you get to know them, they are not anymore." Oh, how that triggered a big reaction! He tried to call me and realized his number was blocked, so he called me from his work number and we started to have a big debate. He was upset at two facts: first that I blocked his number, and second, that I no longer cared for him. I am done with men of his kind for good. He stated that Robert really messed me up and I was scorned.

Until now I never realized it, but I was. And you know what? I am happy to be because before, I thought everyone thought like me, was sincere like I am, and now I am able to see the truth that most people are in it for themselves. That brings me back to the time I was fifteen years old and my views on life were very negative due to all the pain I had endured. I had a look on life like nothing good would last long, because everything good went away as fast as it came. I was sitting in my house on Illinois Avenue, and I had been back home for two years; before that, I was living in a group home.

As I sat in the cold house with no heat in the middle of the winter waiting for my mother to come home, I started to think of my escape plan. My mother was yet again treating me like dog crap, and I was fed up. I told myself once I left this time, it was for good, because if I stayed any longer, someone was going to be dead. I was not sure who it would have been.

As I go through the journal entries I wrote at this time in my life, I come across a section that was written about my feelings and my mother and my life. It read:

Today is December 6, 1993.

I went to school today and had fun. I and my friend Shelly were together. Brenda was mad because Shelly and I were together, but like I said, I don't kiss no one's behind. Today my so-called mother punished me by keeping me off the phone for two months, but that's okay. I know a way to get back at her. At this time I am so mad I could kill her. One day, I can feel it, I am going to explode and don't give a crap how she feels. This lady is trying to make me peanut butter and jelly sandwiches for dinner. I am going to get her for that too. I think she is a freak, a slut, and more, and if she reads my journal, she deserves to know how I feel. I think I am going to leave, not run away, and never come back. I won't tell no one except my boo and never come back to live with her. I know when she gets older, she is going to need me, and I will not be there. In my eyes, I think she is torturing me because of my father. Once I am gone, they would have to kill me first before I ask her for anything. I will hoe for what I need before I ask her for anything. She made my childhood shitty, hateful, and mischievous, and in my life story and when I get older, I am going to let it be known if I am strong enough to get there without doing something drastic, all I have to say is what goes around comes around and when get comes on you, it is the worst. Writing in you will make me feel better for the two months I am punished. I will not play with my little brother or hold a conversation with my sister. I will write later.

As I sit here thinking about life, I had the hardest time sleeping last night. I took this new diet pill, and I just tossed and turned all night. I do not like the feeling this pill gave me, but I do not like the feeling I have with this weight on me either. I remember once catching one of Oprah shows she had a guest on talking about weight and saying that our weight problem is not the food but our relationship with God.

As I sit back, I wonder why every morning I wake up at two or three o'clock and the first thing I do is eat. I do remember a preacher telling me that the Lord wants me to pray and bond with him when I get those urges at night, but instead I think it's my mind telling me to eat. I definitely need to get better eating at night and try to pray and talk to God. I wonder how that will affect my midnight cravings and weight, but most importantly, my relationship with God.

I am hoping that whoever reads this book doesn't get offended by my straightforward approach. I need everyone to understand that all these emotions and feelings I have had have been bottled inside of me and I am tired of feeling stuck. I feel the first approach to real healing is to accept all your inner demons and attack them. As I sit back and reread my journal entries all leading up to when I got married at fifteen and beyond, I should have been a basket case. I get so upset at myself for always being so pure and nice, allowing the most evil people to take advantage of me, giving everyone the benefit of the doubt. I remember how I was so strong the last couple years before I left Marsh once I finally gained control over my own life. It just seems like after Melton, I started revisiting my past. Now that I look at it, Melton was just an accomplishment. I feel I would have withstood mental damage if I had sustained our so-called relationship.

Robert was the closest thing to what a normal relationship is supposed to be like. I loved that feeling. You know, the feeling of feeling normal, no added stress, healthy minds working together. I know I really felt down about the failure of that relationship. It was really hard to lose that relationship because I had finally started to feel that I was getting my reward of true clean love that I was so determined to receive, but for some reason I can't explain, God had other plans for me. I now realize the man for me can't be just any man. He has to be a real man, a man of honor, a man of pride, and a man of God, with the true meaning of faithfulness and strength. I know I need a man who can know all I endured and appreciate me for it and love me even more because of it. Maybe God has to work on Robert a little more before he is ready for me.

But even when I saw no light at the end of my tunnel and no way out, I was still determined. My little sister, who is now twenty-five and married with two kids, just dropped my niece off to me for day care; she and her husband just bought their first house almost two weeks ago. I am so proud of them and their accomplishments. They have a fairy-tale relationship. My sister's husband is the only guy she has ever been with, and they knew each other since the age of fifteen. Get this: they are the same exact age, same birth date, and they are each other's best friends.

I remember before my sister could even think of a boyfriend, Marsh and I had really bad fights. When my little sister was over to my house for the weekend, Marsh would bust my lip for catching him on the phone with another woman. And my little sister witnessed that! I think she was about ten and I was seventeen. I remember getting on my knees and praying to God. I said:

> Dear Jesus, wherever you are, please get me out of this situation. One day allow me to be happy and free, and Jesus, whatever you do when it is time for my sister to get married and learn love, please find the perfect guy for her. Please do not allow her to endure any of my pain and suffering, and if I have to endure more to secure my sister from feeling the way I feel, please protect her and let her future relationship be better than this. Amen, thank you, Jesus.
>
> I remember once I prayed that prayer, I knew my sister was going to be okay. I just felt a feeling of acknowledgment from God. I also knew that one day I was going to be free.

Now fourteen years later, I can actually sit back and reflect on my prayer and thank God for protecting her and me. At my sister's wedding, when it was time for everyone to say something, I got up, and my mother was popping out of her seat, afraid of what I was about to say. I guess it was her guilt that kicked in, especially since we had words earlier on in the dressing room. As I lifted my champagne glass, nervous and shaking, I told the crowd how I prayed to God that my sister would not endure all I had experienced. I can finally say he answered my prayer. I know the audience had no real clue of what I had endured. And my sisters didn't even fully understand either, but because of my beliefs and love for her, an extra blessing was being bestowed over her and her family. As long as I knew my children and little sister were okay, I knew everything I went through was worth it.

Lil Sis, I always tried my best to protect you, even when I did not know I was. Due to the abuse and caseworkers, you were protected from the harsh treatment I received. And even though I was hurt as you and your husband's relationship started to strengthen and ours started to descend, I am now mature enough to know that is was in life plans. As I continue on my life journey, I will continue to pray for your happiness. I just want to ask you not to forget me as you grow and the love I have for you.

As I dig in my past, I am forced to reveal skeletons that I buried and emotions that I hid, but through this I am reminded of how strong I really am and how determined I am not to be hurt by humankind anymore.

Chapter 7

Life is a test. Either we pass, fail, or barely slide through.
I get all As.

Today is Monday, September 01, 2010, and I am riding to Nigeria Springs, New York.

Yesterday was a bitter but sweet day. I went to Paul's Club event, the event was different. Paul had this bright outfit on that was so embarrassing loud. Paul and his outfit along with his big ego was the size of Mount Rushmore that night. From the look of him it totally help me to confirm that I was not interested in him, but for one very small moment after seeing him look like a celebrity, I started to rethink that until reality kicked back in. Being at the event made me feel weird and out of place.

I could not help but rush out of there, before it was over. While there I saw all types of people, and instead of seeing God's children, I felt like I was an soon to be angel trying to get my wings in the devil's pit and everyone was pointing at me and laughing, and then the movie *Carrie* replayed in my head. What have our people turned to? Sex, rocking demonic looks men looking like women and vice versa it seems to be the next best thing to sliced bread. I am not knocking any one religion or sexual origin. Who am I to judge? I embrace everyone, but I do pray God to help his people to see the correct path for the future or we all are doomed.

Besides the crazy event on Sunday, this weekend was good for me. The kids were all gone, and I had the house to myself. Just me and my dogs—what a great feeling. And now I am on my next venture to Niagara Falls.

As I am riding to Niagara Falls, it is raining outside, and Sade is playing on the radio. A sense of peace and tranquility is going through my body and soul, and even if it's just for a moment, I feel peace.

As I sit back and reflect today, my conversation with my friend Carolyn comes into play. Carolyn and I have been friends since ninth grade, and when I talk to her, I can hear the growth and maturity in her voice. There was a big gap where we lost contact with each other due to life situations, but we are now talking again. As I started to read the first couple pages of my book to her, I started to cry. I want to see a therapist to be hypnotized so I can bring up other memories that I know are suppressed in my brain. I know there are memories of more tragic events that are cluttered in my mind. I am so ready to release every secret that I forced myself to hide because I just wanted to be normal; I want to let it out and let it surface. I so want to learn everything about who Alexandria Nolan really is. I am ready to know myself. God has led me to this point to find out.

Yesterday I looked at my calendar to see how long it had been since I called Robert or even contacted him, and it has been three months. A part of me wants to call him and see if any emotions will retrigger. It's like playing Russian roulette with my heart, and even though I feel like I am content with him out my life, a great part of me feels unsure and still wonders if there is still something there. I will try my best not to call, but if I do, you will be the first to know.

Paul has been contacting me saying he wants a baby and family with me. I am into him, but I do find myself daydreaming about that thought with me and Robert. I promise myself to take things slow, so I will. I hope this book is finished before Oprah retires. I want to go on her show so badly. Ever since I was a child, I remember watching Oprah when I was being abused, and she had people on her show that I could relate to. Like the lady Judy. Judy was a woman with multiple personalities. Judy was abused as a child by her father. I used to be like wow, my life was not so bad, but in reality it was. That's when I knew I was not the only one going through stuff. Oprah used to cry and comfort her guest and even revealed her own abuse. From that day forward, I used her strength to get through my pain. I even went to school for broadcasting.

I remember all my peers wanting to be the next Michael Jordan, actress, or rap star.

I wanted to be Oprah, mainly because of her whole well-being; I want to be the next abused woman helping and understanding women of my kind.

The other day was the first time I actually watched her show after years, but Oprah was always in my heart. As I am writing, I look back at my thoughts and memories and see my confusion, pain, and the mistakes I still make on a day-to-day basis. I feel like I am still looking for love in so many places. I just hope as I recognize this, I get stronger in stopping myself from depending on someone else making me happy. I truly want to feel happy just being me and content.

Today is September 27, 2010, and this weekend came with a lot of bumps and surprises. It was bitter.

After getting off the phone with Robert, yes, Robert, I went out for a little while. Our conversation was great, and I can confidently say I am over him. I mean, I still care and have love for him, but I accept that it's over. Things are picking up in my emotional state. I am determined to move at my own pace now and not allow anyone else to dictate the rate at which I will do things. Robert told me he misses me and that I spoiled him and now it's hard for him to find someone because she has to be like me or better. I just smiled and said to myself, good luck trying, because I am definitely one of a kind.

Well, today is Saturday, September 30, 2010, and I am on my way yet again to Niagara Falls. For yet another relaxing road trip. Thursday was a very challenging day. It was one of those bittersweet days that just became more and more ironic as the day progressed.

My little brother, who stands six feet tall and is dark-skinned with a great smile, just recently graduated from high school. And was standing in the grocery line helping me with my groceries. As I stood there in line proud of his accomplishment I start reliving watching him go across the stage, I began to dream of how it would have felt if that were me going across the stage.

While daydreaming of what it may have felt like to have graduated and having my family there this guy named Wes, whom I recently met, a few months back called. I couldn't trust this guy—or any guy—but I didn't mind hanging around him from time to time when I had the time, and he didn't mind spoiling me with gifts and surprises.

Just as I was hanging up the phone, it started to ring again. I looked down, and a 555 number appeared on my caller ID. "Hello," I said as I answered the phone.

"Yes," the voice replied, "how do you know Wes?" *Oh my God*, I thought as I stood there in a state of confusion and disbelief; this had to be a joke. *Why is someone playing a game with me?* I mean, I have not experienced this situation since Melton, and before that, I was the one calling women. I had an excuse at that time. I was young and dumb and married to a freak. *The voice on the other line couldn't even wait until I got my groceries in the car before calling*, I thought to myself.

As I sat there in a state of despair and instant shock, I started to laugh in disbelief. Why did my notions and beliefs have to come true? Why couldn't I just be overreacting for a change as I sat there on the phone with what to me now was the other woman? I was determined to find out the whole story.

The voice continued, "My name is Michelle, and Wes lives with me. This is why at night you can't reach him. I heard the voice mail you left, so what is you guys' relationship?"

Now at this stage in my life, I was all about getting down to the bottom of things. What started as a call out of the blue turned into a day event. I shared with her just what Wes and I were sharing: the money he spent, the time we shared, and even the sexual pleasures he wanted to place on me.

As I sat there listening to this woman, I couldn't even get upset. This situation quickly brought me back to the basket case Tim. Wes was a Gump compared to Tim. As I sat there listening to this lady, the first thing I thought was Tim sure didn't break me, so no runner-up was going to. I was almost lost after Tim. His energy drained me and tarnished my faith a little. To this day I am still rebuilding myself and washing his demons away from me.

After my conversation with Michelle, I was determined to fight the devil once again. I was going to get her to throw his cheating behind out of the house. So I told her everything. We as women have to stick together to stop men from dogging us. I knew she might not keep her end of the bargain, but I was done with his behind.

Once I approached him, he showed his true colors. He started to show me how chemically imbalanced he truly was. He started crying screaming and even had a look of rage. I can tell he was fighting his own demons within his self. Wow, what another basket case I had attracted.

As I live my life, I continue to run across people that make me feel more and more like this world is disrupted and corrupted. After finding this out, I could no longer be around Wes. The sight of him made me upset. I just wanted to harm him to teach him that not every woman is the same and every dog has his day. So I began to ignore his phone calls and move on once again.

I truly feel I am ordained to become a minster one day. I am called to help women prevent themselves from being caught up in dysfunctional relationships and to help them pull out of situations of abuse.

But before I could help people, I had to live it so I would know how to help.

Chapter 8

If you stop trying to control a situation and let the situation take care of itself, things will fix themselves.

Today is November 15, 2010 and today was my uncle's funeral. Things seem so vague right now. I just arrived at the library to have clear mental thoughts, and the librarian almost pissed me off. Besides that, today was yet another bittersweet day. At the funeral I saw so much family people getting older and as I sat there I just imaged that yet one day this very day will be everyone day.

I am actually not afraid of that day. The fear comes in when I feel like I might not leave the legacy God intended for my life, so I feel more eager to do so. Wow, so many faces, so little time, here today, gone tomorrow. Life is like a tricky gift; you receive it, and then it's gone. Memories of my great uncle flushed my mind, and I felt drained because there was so much to say and not the words to say it.

Seeing my grandmother and her only brother left hurts. I know one day my siblings and I will be the same.

As my grandmother's brother sat in his wheelchair in the aisle with only one leg left crying, tears fell down from his eyes. The sadness rushed my bones and tears flooded my eyes like Niagara Falls. I told myself I must make this family even more proud of me. Everyone tells me they are so proud of me and all I've accomplished, but for some reason, I never feel too proud. I guess it's because I want so much more, and then I can feel accomplished.

As I was sitting in the funeral parlor, a voice called to me from my right side. When I turned around, I saw a very familiar face.

I did not know how I should feel. Should I hug that person with thanks and relief, or see this person with sadness and sorrow? I never knew why she did what she did for me. Was it because she truly cared, or was she trying to prove a point to my mother? I will soon get the answers, and until then, I will have unanswered emotions.

"You promise not to tell my mom?"

"Yes," the voice replied as I sat in her bedroom scared of what my mother would do if she found out that I was telling someone of the abuse she had inflicted on me. I was eight years old at the time and was talking to my mom's friend Jenifer.

"Mommy hits me a lot," I vaguely remember telling her, "and she says she hates my lips because they remind her of my daddy. Are my lips big to you? Mommy beats me for reasons I don't know. I love Mommy, but I am scared that one day she may kill me."

Jenifer listens to me cry out and starts to ask me questions in detail about the abuse I endured.

As I start to tell her, all I can remember was fear that my mommy was going to find out and really beat me, but Jenifer promised not to tell so I trusted her. I mean, she had her own issues as a mom, so this was just going to be our little secret. Some secret.

A week after telling Jenifer this, I missed school on one not-so-happy day. My mother seemed very frustrated due to bills and work when I woke up that morning. As I prepared for school, my mother was very snappy. "Do this, do that," she screamed. As I started tying my shoes, "Don't look at me. Just tie your damn shoes," she hollered. As I proceeded to look up trying to figure out why she was mad, the spray-can bottle of spray starch smacked my face. I jumped up crying out of shock and pain, grabbing my face. My mother looked down and was shocked herself to see that her actions caused my face to be bruised and cut.

My mother refused to send me to school that day due to a prior incident a year earlier. She iced my face and gave me candy and told me when I returned to school to explain to them my little sister, who was two at the time, did it. I sat there eating my candy, loving the attention I was receiving since it was very rare.

But when I returned to school, the sight of my eye prompted the school to call Social Services and before you knew it, Social Services was rushing in. That day was so scary to me. One moment I was being drilled at school by this strange lady, and the next they were pulling me into the government car. As I was being placed in the car, all I could see was my mother pulling up, wondering why I had not arrived home from school and seeing me getting escorted into the car. "Mommy," I started to cry, "I want my mommy."

As I am writing this, I just figured it out. I allowed people who did bad things in my life because I thought of it as love. Mommy loved me, right? And she hurt me. Maybe that was everyone's way of showing their love to me as a child. Wow, I was really screwed up as a child.

And the crazy thing now is I see my mom, but I do not know how to love her. How could I love her now that I am grown, knowing what it is to be a mom? I could not do my children the way she did me. Why, Mom, why did you hurt me and never apologize for the pain? I was so young and innocent, and I really loved you. You were my mother.

As we sat in the repast room waiting for everyone to come back from the cemetery, I met one of my cousins, who is also a singer and film producer. I got reacquainted with my cousin Tabatha and many family members, and I sat beside my lovely grandmother, who I pray doesn't pass away anytime soon.

Tabatha hugged me and congratulated me on being strong and overcoming the odds. I so badly wanted to talk to her in detail, but I could see my mother in the corner of my eye, afraid of what I might say to degrade her. I just thought to myself, *Wow, Mom, I hope you can handle the truth of this book when I finish it. I am not trying to hurt you. I just want to be free, I just want to be free.* My dad called me the other day; he knew I was disappointed. I just nodded my head. Of the two parents God picked for me on earth, both had great talents and both had a child without the true meaning of loving me. I may one day make you both proud, but when will I get the day to be proud of both of you?

It hurts to never know the feeling of a daddy's love and a mother's readiness. I did not ask for you to be my parents. Why don't you love me? I wanted to ask them both. I love my children and would not ever want to take them back.

I don't care who their daddy is. I am their mommy, so they are mine. So why couldn't you guys love me that way? And I wanted to reach out to Robert and say, "Don't be afraid. My kids are the reflection of being raised the right way."

Uncle Field, even though you passed away and left us here, today I have gained a legacy of love and patience. I want you to know I always loved and admired your fatherhood and your love for Aunt Kate. And I know you will rest in peace. I pray one day to have a man in my life with the love and endurance you displayed to your children and kids. Even though I was young and not around much, I saw you be a very healthy man and father and husband. Even though I was faced with different parents, you helped show me that there was a better way, and through this, I will not give up.

After saying farewell to my uncle, I was very curious what it felt like to die and what death really felt like. I am not ready to pass. I just wondered what Uncle Field felt when he left, and was he truly with his three siblings, both his parents, and his grandson. I wondered if he was at peace. I no longer wanted to see death as a bad thing, but more like a step we take once we have done what God set us on earth for.

Once I arrived home and searched the web for near-death experiences, just as I thought, there were people who admitted to seeing the other side. It was so calm and pure, with family members that had passed before. After hearing their experiences, I knew Uncle Field was at peace. And all the loved ones he left behind were to. Before I am ready to join them, I have to be at peace with myself and proud of Alexandria. And most importantly, I have to touch the lives of many people with my light and save some lost souls.

Through every mistake, there is a lesson and a sense of growth. Writing this book is like therapy to me. I am able to expose all my hidden walls and free my soul. Once I finish this book, I am going to go through all my journal entries and burn them. I know I am on the right path now. I have been on it; I just became blinded along the way. God is good. My cousin Tabatha said something that made me realize she too felt like what I endured as a child was way too much. She looked and me and whispered I am so proud of you, you were always a loving child I just wish I was able to help you. I looked up at her and smiled. The deepness in my eyes spoke a thousand words and we sat there and ate our food at the repast. Besides the abuse with my mom, there was the continued abuse I received from the age of fifteen until twenty-three from my husband and cousin. And to think my great uncle who just passed was Marsh's grandfather's nephew.

Sometimes when I shared my story to certain people, they still felt I was old enough to know what love was at such a young age. All except this guy named Mike.

Mike was a cool guy. We were strictly acquaintances. I had no attraction to him, but we had great conversation. After sharing a little bit of my life story and letting him understand why there was a wall up, he was horrified by the fact I was married young, and even more upset that Marsh was in his twenties, with three kids already. "Who let this happen?" he said. "You were just a baby." And he was right. I was a baby, the same exact age my older daughter is today, and she plays video games, talks on the phone, and only gets on the computer with parental supervision. Just think: at her very age, I was pregnant by a twenty-three-year-old man with three kids, who cheated and abused me physically and mentally for the first three years after having our first child. Where were the people whom I needed the most?

Chapter 9
(A Child's Cry)

Visions of my past flood my heart; the innocence of my soul was broken.

The next few chapters are the hardest to write about, and as I sit back and think about how to tell my story, I start to go through anxiety and pain all over again. Tears rush into my eyes, but I refuse not to tell my story. It must be told; it must be said.

My mother was about seventeen years old. My father was much older. I remember my mother telling me that she packed her bags one day when I was about eight months old and left my father for good. Growing up, I never had a dad. The closest thing I had to a father was my sister's father, but he only lasted for a short time. I was told I was a bundle of joy. From the time I was nine months old, I was already walking, drinking out of a cup, and using the potty.

I was a happy child, but all that changed when my mother had my little sister. Once my sister was born and things did not work out with her father, my mother started to show her frustration—her frustration with life, and especially her frustration toward men. And it all started to become her frustration toward me as well.

After Social Services took me from my mother the first time, you would have thought she would have learned. I remember us catching the bus to counseling and going to check in with my caseworker. I was starting to feel safe. But once my mother dotted all her I's and crossed all her T's, my caseworkers closed the case. Then my real mother came out again. We went through this for almost eight years, her beating me and me getting taken away and then sent back to her. As I got older, I started gaining the guts to stand up to her.

I remember the time my mother read my journal after I wrote a fake situation about a boy and me kissing. I had just copied that story from a kids' show and wrote the same scenario in my journal. I guess she was bored or looking for something because she went in my room and read my journal. When I got home from school, I didn't know what I was getting into. As I opened the front door, my pregnant mother's eyes were furious. I was confused.

"Bitch, what the fuck is this?" she yelled as she proceeded to reach for my hair and pull me to the ground. I was thirteen years old at the time.

"What did I do?" I screamed as she pulled my hair against the weight bench.

"This," she yelled, throwing my journal.

"Mom, it was a lie. I made it up."

My mother's boyfriend came into the room and pulled her off me. "Stop! Get off that girl," he yelled.

My mother turned from me to him. She yelled out, "Mind your damn business or get the fuck out."

"I hate you," I screamed, running out the front door with no shoes and nowhere to go.

It was cold. I was scared, but I'd rather take a chance on the street than go back to that house. After twenty minutes of contemplating, my street smarts kicked in, and I ran six blocks around the corner to my aunt's house, crossing three main streets barefoot and all. Once I got to my aunt's house, she consoled me and then called my mother. My aunt yelled at her about me being in the streets of DC at night and without a coat or shoes.

My mother's response was, "Alex is strong. I knew she was going to figure it out."

My aunt hung up the phone, and we talked and I slept the night there.

After running for what I believed was my life, the rebellious stage of my life started. I started to have the mind-set of if I was going to get hit or in trouble anyway, I might as well make it worth it.

A few weeks passed. I was back home and everything was normal.

One of my responsibilities was to go pick my little sister up from day care about five blocks away and bring her home after my school let out. So just like any other day, I went home first, dropped off my book bag, and then left to go on my daily walk to get my little sister. Walking was fun to me; it was the only time I felt free. I never went anywhere or had friends come over, so walking to get my sister was the closest thing to freedom I had. Other than that, I had a military schedule. It went like this: 6:00 dress; 8:30–3:00 school; 4:00 chores, dinner, and homework; 8:00 bed; no TV time, no phone time, no nothing. It was terrible.

Well, as I was walking to the day care, a boy came up beside me and said, "Hello."

"Are you talking to me?" I replied as I turned around to see the face of the person trying to get my attention.

"Yep," he replied. "There is no one else around."

I looked around and laughed. "I guess you're right," I replied. And I started to blush. *Wow*, I thought, *someone is taking an interest in me and he is my age*. Before this, every male that tried to come on to me was a grown-up. But this time it felt normal; it felt right.

"My name is Quoin," he said.

I was so scared. *Is this really true?* I wondered. Before you knew it, Quoin was meeting me every day to walk with me to pick up my little sister. I would call him every day before I left the house, and we would meet up. I knew eventually he would want more than to just walk with me, but I did not want to rush things, and besides I was on lockdown. Two weeks passed, and he asked me to be his girlfriend. I said yes, but I had no clue what I was getting into. How on earth was I going to be able to really be his girlfriend when my mother was so strict?

Things did not get better at home. My mother was getting meaner by the day. The man she was pregnant by and the only guy that took up for me had packed his things and left. I was dazed, depressed, and failing school. Every day I would go to school, but I could not concentrate on my work. I did not understand the teachers or the assignments. Nothing was clear, my brain was cluttered, and I was cracking inside. Quoin's face was the only thing that kept me going, but I knew that would end soon because eventually he would want more and I could not give it to him. *In April 1992, when I was fourteen, Quoin gave me something that would change my life; what once had looked to me as untouchable was now in my reach. My eyes opened to the real world. A world with no emotions or a gunshot with no mark, all started to change to an open wound with no explanation and a heart with so much pain the gunshot started to bleed and the world looked insane. My total innocence was cleared out of my eyes, and I saw the truth.*

I was walking from my friend Kaye's house. We walked to school together every day, but on this particular day, she was playing hooky. Alex I am not going to school today. Kaye said as she looked across the street. I am hanging out at LW. LW is what we called the area were Quoin and Bradley lived.

"Girl, you know Quoin and Bradley. For real, I asked as I looked in her eyes for confirmation. but if my mother finds out I cut school, I'm going to be dead." I followed up.

Kaye quickly turn her eyes from where LW was and looked at me as she stated "Girl, you're going to be dead anyway."

After she stated that, I thought to myself she was right. Regardless of what I did I got in trouble, so why not make my pain worth it? At least I had something to look forward to. At least now I would have some friends.

So I cut school and went to Bradley's house. Bradley was older than us. He was a high school dropout and had a fun house. Everyone would go over there to cut school, drink, watch movies, and just chill. Once I got there, I was scared. Quoin came to me and grabbed my hand. We talked for a while, and then he said he wanted to spend time alone with me. My heart started to race like I was running in the Olympics. I had never been with Quoin alone—or any boy. Everything was so new to me. As we sat in the room, we started to talk.

"Are you a virgin?" he asked.

I paused for a second and thought back to all the times there had been men in my life, men I looked up to as a father figure, and then I remembered the time I played house with my mother's best friend's son. "No," I replied. But I really was.

He started to lean toward me. I did not like it; my stomach started to get tight, and I was starting to feel sick. *No, Quoin, please do not be like the others*, I thought silently to myself. I tried to convince myself this must be right. It was legal; we were the same age. I silently screamed stop, but a part of me wanted him to go on. If someone were going to take my virginity, I wanted it to be someone I chose, and certainly not a grown man.

So I let Quoin do to me what everyone else had tried to accomplish. I cried. The pain was bad, but the beatings I received were worse.

Quoin looked at me and wiped my tears. "You lied," he said. "You were a virgin."

All I could think was that my mother had told me not to do it, but I did and it was my life. From that day on, I took control of my life and who was going to hurt me. I soon learned how to walk with no emotions and have a bleeding heart without a patch. The innocent little girl was now standing up for herself.

— *Chapter 10* —

I once experienced pain without the benefit of gain.
I once experienced love without the benefit of purpose.
I once experienced life without the benefit of dying.
I once experienced death without the benefit of living.

Cutting school was starting to be a habit, but the teachers started calling my mom and telling her I missed school. She would come to me and fuss, but I started to get guts and stand up to her. I was no longer going to sit back and let her talk to me any ol' way. I had no clue that life was about to take another turn, and my view about boys was about to change even more.

The day seemed like any other day I played hooky, but as I was going into Bradley's house, my neighbor's daughter saw me.

"Alex, what are you doing around here?"

I looked up and it was Wanda. *Oh man*, I thought. I quickly ran down the steps and out the door. I prayed she wouldn't tell my mother. I was hoping she would spare me. I mean, she knew the abuse I was going through; she had even witnessed it firsthand. When I was about ten years old and my mother got mad at me because I got my hair messed up and lost my barretts, my mother literally pulled me by my hair, grabbing my pigtail as we crossed the busy streets leaving the after-care center I used to go to. I was screaming and crying, and when we turned the corner, all the neighborhood kids were standing there watching me being dragged down the street by my ponytail. It was so humiliating. Wanda's mother just shook her head, but Wanda herself jumped in and tried to get my mother off my hair. "Stop, Margret, you're hurting the girl," she yelled. It was like my mother blanked out. So why would Wanda tell her? I thought she knew what I was facing.

Wanda even witnessed the time my sister bit me and I hit her back. Before I could turn my back, my mother charged me on the steps and started upper cutting me. Once I ran down the steps I went to school, but it felt weird because I was lost in my classes and did not understand the work. I really wanted to succeed in school, but I felt like I was behind too much. I had nowhere to turn, and my mother was the worst to ask for help. She would get frustrated and knock me upside the head, so I just shut down.

I kept cutting school. Quoin and I did not have sex anymore, mainly because I did not like it. If sex felt like that, why was everyone rushing to do it? I started thinking both Quoin and I didn't know what we were doing or sex was stupid. But I was not interested in finding out which one it was. The school kept calling, Almost two weeks had passed since I last ran in to Wanda I was starting to believe that maybe Wanda didn't tell, but one day when I went to Bradley's house and Quoin and I were chilling with everyone else, watching movies and laughing, there was a knock at the door. No one was surprised; we thought maybe it was the neighbors complaining about the noise—they were good at that.

Once Bradley opened the door, I turned to see who it was. To my surprise, it was my mother and my sister's father standing there. My heart dropped, and I knew I would never see Quoin again.

"Come on, Alexandria," my mother said.

I started to cry, and I looked at Quoin as I walked out the door. The ride home seemed like forever, but it was only two blocks away.

Once we arrived home, I prepared myself for a beating. My sister's father sat on the couch with me and I felt safe, but once he made sure my mother was fine, he kissed me on the head and started to walk out the door.

I jumped off the couch and ran to him. "Please don't leave me here with her," I begged, pulling on his clothes. "She's going kill me."

"No, she isn't," he replied. "You will be safe."

Who the hell did he think he was leaving me with—the Virgin Mary? *This lady is nowhere near safe*, I thought.

Minutes after he left, the front door opened again, and I jumped up feeling relieved. I said, "Thanks. You came back," but it was not him anymore. It was my social worker, Mrs. Mateo. Not only was my mother not beating me; she was giving me up to the state. And to make matters worse, Bradley started spreading rumors about me saying we slept together, so Quoin was mad at me. From that day on, I looked at all males the same, boys or men, and promised not to have sex again.

As I was riding in the state-appointed car yet again, I just stared in a glaze out the window. I was numb. Mrs. Mateo was nice when I was younger, but I was getting tired of her face. We had been down this road too many times. I just looked out the window at the poor city streets and watched the bums and the bag ladies walk and beg. I prayed that God would find a way to get me out of this city and slump. I always grew up in a house, and we moved six different times and I went to eight different schools in the city. I used to wonder why every time I got used to my friends, my mother would up and move and I had to meet new friends. I was so burned out of the same thing.

Mrs. Mateo and I arrived at this weird-looking house. I got confused. It was nothing like the precinct where she dropped me off last time. The precinct was cold, and I felt like a criminal there. I had to take my clothes off while they took pictures of my body and the bruises, which were purple and blue. Yeah, this place was different, but it was just as scary. It was an old house that looked like a doctor's office on the outside. We went in, and she took me to the office section.

"Alexandria, you will stay here for the night, and they will place you in the morning."

I started to cry. What in the hell was this?

Once Mrs. Mateo left, I was on my own. They took me to the intake section and asked me all types of questions. I was being placed as a ward of the court, and I was just another number now. Once they finished processing me, I was sent to the sitting area with many other kids. I looked at them and nodded my head; if there was one thing about me, I was street-smart so I knew how to fit in. While we sat there waiting for the next step, I overheard the kids there talking about sex, how they had anal sex and liked it, how they had caught STDs. The conversations were getting worse, and I was in shock. What the hell was anal sex? What were STDs? I just promised God if he got me through this, I was going to be a born-again virgin.

The next morning, they gathered me and two other girls, and we went in a van. "Where are we going?" I asked the counselor.

She smiled and replied, "To your new home."

I just sat back. As we arrived at what was said to me to be my new home, it looked much warmer than the place I was just at. As I climbed the many steps to get to the front door, I was like, *this place is pretty neat looking, at least on the outside*. I proceeded to open the door and walk in the house. The house was huge, with four levels inside. There was a living room and dining area and many girls. I began to get nervous because everyone was real teenagers; I was the youngest.

"You know this spot is only for teen girls; she is too young," the lady told the counselor who was dropping me off.

"I know, but they are full everywhere else and she can't stay at Sasha Bruce's. That's an intake/outtake spot," the counselor responded. "I have two more young girls coming in later to drop off, and you guys will hold them until Fourteenth Street is ready for them," she added. The counselor then turned to me and said, "Bye, Alexandria, you will be okay."

I waved good-bye and sat on the couch in the living area. Later, after dinner, they showed me to my room and introduced me to my roommate. *Wow, my roommate is tall*, I thought. She stood about five feet ten inches, and I only stood four-nine. My roommate gravitated to me very well. "You're my little daughter," she said while she was brushing her weave. I smiled.

Chapter 11

A book is not a book without words.
Words are not words without meaning.
Meaning is not meaning without purpose.
Purpose is not purpose without a gift.
A gift is a token from love.
Love is nothing without a heart that was broken.

Staying in the group home did not turn out to be bad after all. I had more freedom than I'd ever experienced. At the group home, we were able to go outside and go places as long as we let the counselor on duty know the area we were at and be back by our curfew, which was eight o'clock for me and nine o'clock for the older girls. We basically could do what we wanted as long as we respected the house and followed the rules. We even got paid five dollars a week for chores and forty dollars a month for a clothes allowance. It wasn't a lot, but it was something. Coming from getting and doing nothing, I was happy. I did not let my freedom go to my head. I followed all the rules and came back on time. I was not going boy-crazy because I was still scorned after my experience with Quoin, plus I made a promise to God.

A couple weeks passed, and my mother and I had not talked. She called the group home, but I was not there. When she found out we were able to go outside and travel, she demanded the counselors keep me in. The counselors smirked at my mother's demand and told her I was a ward of the court and she had no rights to me. I laughed inside, trying to imagine my mother's face when she finally lost control of me. She thought she was teaching me a lesson, and for real, she did. By giving me to the state and them placing me in a group home, I learned a sense of self-pride.

I didn't have to sneak to live my life, I just had to earn it. So the last month of school before the summer kicked in, I went to school each day and passed. I walked past Quoin's way every day, but I stopped looking for him. I wanted to succeed, and now I had control.

After a month passed, the other two new girls came. They were eleven and twelve. I was like their big sister. It didn't take long before they moved us to our own house for girls our age. But the best part was it was only us three that lived there. The girl Selma—she was eleven years old—and I got real close. We shared a room. I always tried to keep them on a positive path. Selma was a virgin, and so was the other girl. So I talked to them about my experience and how boys only wanted one thing. The girls seemed to listen to me. But stuff changed for the worse once a new girl arrived.

The new girl was my age, and she was fast. She was no virgin; she talked about sex all the time. Not even a week after she came, she slept with the older cousin of the boy across the street. I was so embarrassed because they knew our house was a group home and I did not want us to be labeled as hoes. The boy across the street and I were friends, but I never let our friendship get past a walk in the park. Yeah, he wanted more—what boy doesn't? Until I was ready to experience that awful feeling they call sex again, I chose to pass on the offer.

Everything was running smoothly until one day I went to visit my grandmother on a weekend pass. I found out that while I was gone Mrs. Sted, the counselor, took the girls on an outing to the dollar movie. We used to go somewhere every weekend if we didn't have a weekend pass or was not on restriction. The new girl was on restriction that weekend because she skipped curfew to go be with some boys. I was the only one gone on a weekend pass, so Chevron, the girl who moved to the house with Selma, and Selma were the only two who went on the outing, but they were not alone.

Ray, the boy that liked me from across the street, went with them. When I got back home, the new girl came in my room and started telling me about how Selma and Ray were kissing and holding hands at the movie. The new girl explained that Chevron witnessed it all and told her. I was furious—not at Ray because he was being a typical boy; I was so glad I didn't break my promise to myself and God. But I was angry at Selma for betraying me and being fast. I quickly charged her in the phone room. I lifted my hand and slapped her so fast, and then I restrained myself and went in my room. What was I mad for? She wasn't my friend right, and if she wanted to be easy, that was her life. I called Ray and told him to never call me again. He came outside and tried to talk, but I refused to entertain him. Days in the house were never the same, and I was ready to leave.

It wasn't until a week later that Ray caught me outside and apologized. I accepted his apology because I no longer wanted to be his friend and there was no purpose to beef with a guy who lived directly across from me. As he started to express to me his deepest apology, I looked up and saw three girls approaching me. Confused about what was going on and a block away from my house, I felt stuck.

"Who is this, Ray?" the girls asked.

"Tell them your name," Ray said to me.

"I am Alex," I responded with a frown. Then I turned to Ray and told him I was going home.

"Let me buy you some fries from the store," he suggested as he jumped on his bike and rode beside me.

"Okay," I agreed, so Ray and I walked away from the girls toward the carryout.

Before I could even get a block away, I felt someone pull me from behind and knock me to the ground. Out of shock, I started to laugh, thinking it was Ray's friend Fenny, who was also walking with the girls. We used to play-wrestle all the time. "Fenny, you play too much," I screamed jumping up, but as I opened my eyes and looked down, I saw the shoes of one of the girls behind me.

I quickly jumped up and swung. "Bitch," I screamed as I punched her with all my strength. I had been pushed on the ground too much where I couldn't hit back; I definitely was going to defend myself now. After I hit the girl, her sisters jumped and started surrounding me. I was prepared to take on all three. Fenny jumped in and said there was not going to be a jump. The girls started to walk away. As I stood there in shock tears started streaming down my eyes. I was furious. I started to laugh and Fenny turned to look at me what's funny he replied? I looked at Fenny and wiped my face. Then I sent Fenny to tell the girls to come back and fight me one-on-one.

I ran to Upshur Swimming Pool and got Chevron and Selma to have my back just in case they tried to jump me. Everyone met back up blocks from my house, and even more people showed just to watch the fight.

As the girl and I stood face-to-face, I couldn't help but notice she was pretty. I later found out that her name was Nita and she was Ray's girlfriend. "Hit me now," I yelled at her. We went back and forth on who was going to hit first. She started to talk a lot of trash, and I blanked out and stole her in the face. We fought for what seemed to be an hour, both of us getting in good hits. The fight did not break up until an older guy in a cab jumped out of his cab and stopped us.

Weeks after the fight, rumors were going on in the house that Selma and Chevron knew the girls were going to jump me and were watching in the bushes, and they ran back to the pool once the fight was over. Chevron and Selma denied it, but my time was counting down anyway I had been in the group home for four months and I was going back home.

Chapter 12

I am a passenger on this thing called life, and I will wear my seat belt.

The new school year came around, and I was home with my mother. I was not happy, but the group home experience was getting old. I did have hope that my mother was going to finally learn from her mistakes and allow our relationship to blossom. I was older now, and she had to accept it. Just like before, she did not change for long; instead of her abusing me physically, she turned to mental abuse. I remember the time she jumped in my face and said, "On your sixteenth birthday, we are going to fight." I made a promise to myself that on my sixteenth birthday, I was going to be gone for good.

At this time, we moved uptown near the group home, and I was enrolled in the neighborhood junior high school. I had to make new friends all over, but that was not hard. I quickly became popular and earned respect from everyone at the school. I was labeled a tomboy by the way I dressed and the way I carried myself. I always had a curvy shape and was not accepting of it. I hated how older people confused my age by the size of my thighs, so dressing in big clothes was very comfortable for me.

A boy named Derrick caught my eye. We were a lot alike. I was a bad girl, and he was a bad boy. We were both short. Derrick and I dated for a year before I even thought about kissing him. I was serious about my promise. Plus I wanted Derrick to like me for me and respect me, so rushing things would only mess up our relationship. By summertime I was stuck in the house and had no outlet; Derrick and I barely saw each other.

One morning the phone rang, and it was Selma contacting me out of the blue. She said she was staying with her aunt until her sister got custody of her. She asked if she could come and stay with me and my mother for a week until the papers went through. To my surprise, my mother agreed. Shortly after Selma came over, we went in my room and talked. Selma had changed. She was no longer a virgin. As a matter of fact, she had slept with over fifteen boys and thought she was pregnant. I was so disappointed in her. She was only twelve.

A week passed, and Selma had to leave. I decided I was going to go with her. I had twenty dollars to my name, so we caught the bus to her sister's house. My mother had no clue where I was. Again, I had no clue what I was getting into. Selma's sister lived in Southeast. That part of DC was totally different from uptown. When we arrived, I was excited and going through a terrible culture shock at the same time. And to think, I thought I was poor.

Selma's sister's house was terrible. As soon as I walked in, I rushed to the bathroom to spit up. I asked Selma, "What am I getting into?" The house was dirty, and there were beer cans, liquor bottles, old cigarette butts, and dirty diapers all over the living room. In the bedroom there were dirty clothes on the bed. There was spit-up in the hall, and crayon and ink marks on the walls. Every inch of the house was unlivable. Roaches flooded the apartment. I looked at Selma and said, "We can't stay here unless we clean it." So Selma and I blocked the kitchen off with a mattress and cleaned the whole entire apartment.

By nighttime her sister still had not come home, so Selma and I removed the mattress blocking the kitchen to clean it. As I opened the refrigerator, there were maggots swirling around the fridge. The stove had old dirty pots and maggots coming out of the trash. Selma and I looked at each other and put the mattress back. We took a shower and got dressed.

Once we left the house, Selma told me to follow her lead. I looked at her like, wow, this is not the same little girl that looked up to me; she was a woman with childlike qualities. As I stated before, Selma was only twelve, but if you ever met her, you would think she was at least seventeen. Selma had the body of a woman; her butt was three times bigger than mine, and in the city of DC, boys and men went crazy over females with big behinds. I had a nice shape myself, but Selma had too much butt for a twelve-year-old. Selma and I started to walk up the dark streets of Southeast. A guy was coming out of the building to my left. Selma tugged on my shirt and said, "That's Charles. Let's see what he's doing tonight."

The guy looked at Selma and started to walk toward a car with another guy in it. The guy in the car started to call Selma and me over toward the car. I refused to come because this was strange. Selma walked over there and started to chat with them. I looked at Selma and started to regret coming with her. She had made it seem like her sister was a great person, but from the looks of it, her sister was a dirty hood rat. "Come on, Alex," she said as she walked with Charles. "We are going to his house."

I was furious; I didn't want to go. I didn't know what or who was over there. I just dragged behind Selma because I really had no choice. Where was I going to go—back home?

Once we got to Charles's house, it was clean. I felt a little comfortable, but then Charles offered us some liquor. I refused. I was not going to allow myself to lose control. I remember the first time and only time I had drunk liquor; it had not mixed well. My mother's crazy coworker's sister gave it to me. They were teaching me how to play spades, and they gave me a forty to myself. I was so drunk I got into an argument with them because she assumed I started flirting with her boyfriend. What the hell do you think's going to happen if you give alcohol to a minor? So just like sex, drinking was not an option for me.

Selma sat on Charles's bed drinking, and I just tried to concentrate on the television. As I tried to focus on the television I couldn't help but look at all the pictures around Charles house. Pictures of what seem to be his children and his girlfriend. I just stop looking because it started reminding me of all the men who either abused or tried to abuse me. There was one picture of a girl my age with Charles I just could not ignore. Who is that I asked Charles while pointing to the picture? That's my daughter Charles replied. Oh I replied as my silent tears started to form, what a pervert I thought to myself. After his response all I remember was turning my head and balling up in the corner and trying to fall asleep, but when I opened my eyes, Charles and Selma were having sex. I shook my head and ran out of the room.

"Come on, Alex. You know you want some," Charles yelled. The sight of seeing Selma bent over having sex was way too much for me to see. And to think this guy was a grown-ass man with kids the same age as Selma made it worse. I was really ready to leave and go back to the roach-infested apartment after this. Hours passed and by dawn me and Selma left Charles apartment and went back to her sister house. Who was not there yet again.

The next day was a little better, well, the morning at least. My money was running low, and Selma and I were hungry. We went to the 7-Eleven and got something to eat, and then we walked around the neighborhood just talking about our times at the group home.

As we were walking, a black car pulled up beside us. The guy on the driver's side yelled out, "Hey, shorty, come here."

Selma yelled, "That's Blue the guy Charles was taking too from last night," and jumped in the car.

I kept walking. Even if I had to stand out here all day and night, I was not going in his car. They started to follow me.

"Come on, Alex," Selma shouted. "We're just going to McDonald's."

"Man, Selma!" I shouted. "I am going home." but I couldn't leave Selma alone, so I jumped in the car and held extra tight to the handles of the door just in case I had to jump out. As we drove past McDonald's, I yelled out, "Excuse me, McDonald's is that way."

Blue had pulled up in the parking lot of an apartment complex. All I could think of was running, but I had to help Selma out; she was only twelve and making some very dumb choices. "I just got to get something, and then we're going to McDonalds's," Blue replied.

When we entered the apartment, there was this big black dog standing there. I instantly froze.

There was also a guy coming from the back. He looked at me and started to smile. I frowned at him. "Come here; I'm not going to bite," he said.

"Where's your bathroom at?" I asked and then grabbed Selma. She and I walked into the bathroom. "Selma! What the hell are you doing?" I whispered. "We can leave."

"I am okay," she said. "He's going to take us to McDonald's. We're just going to talk."

I looked at Selma and she looked confident in her decision, so I told her to scream if she needed me. We walked out of the bathroom. Selma went into Blue's room, and I sat in the kitchen talking to the other dude.

As I sat there quiet, the guy started to pull on my arm. I snatched it away.

"Back off," I told him firmly.

He responded, "While you're in here playing Mrs. Good Girl, they're back there getting it in. We can be doing that; come on."

"Boy, I don't know you," I screamed, "and if that's what they choose to do, that's them." I looked at the boy again and I said, "You look familiar." And instantly I realized where I knew him from. "You used to be in Hyattsville?" I asked him.

"Yep," he replied.

"Well, you were throwing apples at me and my friends a year ago," I replied. He gave me a confused face. "Well, when Selma and I were in the group home, the counselor would take the girls with them to go grocery shopping. While the counselors were shopping, I and the other girls walked around the neighborhood. On one particular day, we were walking around, and some guys started screaming at us. I yelled back, 'That's disrespectful,' and they started throwing apples from the apple tree that was growing in the yard. I remember looking up at them, and your face stayed in my memory as we started laughing and running back to the grocery store."

"Yep, that was me," the guy laughed.

We both looked at each other and laughed as Selma was coming out of the room. Selma looked like she was in shock. I jumped up and looked at Blue and gave him a real mean mug.

I grabbed Selma's arm and pushed her in the bathroom. "What's the matter?" I asked.

"He raped me," Selma responded.

I replied, "I'm going to go out there and tell him how old you are, and we are going to call the police."

"No, Alex," Selma responded. "He's crazy. Let's just get out of here safely."

It took all my strength to say nothing, I was so mad. I was mad at Selma for putting us in this situation. I was angry at myself because I couldn't do anything. I didn't even say good-bye to the other guy as we were leaving. I grabbed Selma and made her sit in the back with me.

"Why you sitting back there?" Blue asked her.

"I want her too," I replied. "You already got what you wanted."

Selma looked at me and shook her head.

"Well, he did," I replied.

Blue did at least keep his word and took us to McDonalds. I ordered my meal and Selma ordered hers. After we got our food, I looked at Blue and told him, "We don't need a ride, we can walk." I had refused to get back in his car. Blue looked at me and gave me a smirk and drove off.

Selma and I walked back to the neighborhood where her sister lived. I ate my food while we walked; Selma just held her food and dazed off. Once we got back around the neighborhood, there were some guys standing on the corner.

They saw Selma's food and snatched it. They said *Assalamu alaikum* and started eating her food. They had this weird pact going on around there that if you wanted to keep your food when you brought it on the strip, you had to say *salaka salam* or someone could snatch it. I guess Selma was dazed out and forgot.

I shouted, "Stop, give it back."

They paid me no attention. I wanted to say, "You don't know what she had to go through to get that."

Two days passed, and this street life was wearing on me. Selma Sister showed up just as we were leaving out. She looked half drunk and tried so I didn't get a chance to really meet her. As me and Selma walked out of the apartment I couldn't help but wonder rather I wanted to stay here any longer all the guys around there would come to me and say abruptly, "You don't fit in around here; go home." And they were right.

As Selma and I sat on the steps of this apartment complex just chilling, the guy we called Reese came up.

"Hey, little shorty, hold this," he said.

When I looked down, it was a gun. "Nah," I said, shaking my head.

"Just for a minute," he replied. "The popo hot out here today," he added, "and they won't check yah."

Selma looked at me and said, "If you going to hang on these streets, you gotta be loyal."

So Reese put the gun in my back and walked off. Reese was known around there and he knew the police was going to target him. So he needed me to hold his what the call peacemaker until they left. Later I learned the gun was a.32 caliber. An hour passed, and just like Reese said, the police were out that day. I had seen at least five police car patrolling the area.

As I sat there tying my shoes, I looked up, and a lady was walking up the steps. She got to the top and stood right in front of me. Hold up; she looked familiar.

"It's her," she said, yelling to the person at the bottom at the steps.

I did a double-take, and it was my mother's friend. At the bottom was my mother, and standing next to her was a police car. For the first time, I truly was happy to go home.

I had no time to put away the gun, everything was happening so fast. They took Selma and me to the police precinct. I was scared. *I had a gun on me*. Selma and I both went to the bathroom and tried to figure out things. We both agreed it would be better I took the gun with me since she was going to be there until they found somewhere for her to go. Wow I was actually in the police precinct with a hand gun and no one knew. The police released me into my mother's custody and we left. Selma was stuck at the precinct until her aunt came later that night.

Chapter 13

Emotions are like fish in a deep blue sea: they can get thrown out there and then lost in a whole lot of motion where no one cares about them.

Back home and back to reality. Selma and I lost contact again. Last I heard she was pregnant, but I didn't have time to care. I just knew if I ever ran away again. it was going to be for good. And it was not going to be with Selma.

School time came back around, and I was entering high school. I was very upset because that summer the school system changed the rules and put all ninth graders in high school. I was unprepared; I wanted a ninth-grade prom and a graduation. All was robbed from me over the summer due to the change. Derrick and I were still doing fine but he was turning me off because he dropped out of school to sell drugs and all he cared about was the street, so I started to pull myself and my emotions away from him.

After school I would go home and do my homework and maybe talk on the phone to my cousin Marsh. Marsh and I had just met a couple months earlier. He was much older than I. He seemed real cool, though. Marsh was still living at his parents' house, but he was telling me about how his job offered him an apartment and if he got it, I could come live there and go to school from there. Everything sounded real, and I started to plan my escape.

Before I made the final decision to leave, I wanted to be certain it was the right choice. So I promised myself to try to give my mother and me another chance. I came home, did all my chores, took care of my siblings, and even cooked dinner. But my mother still was not happy. Christmas time came, and as my siblings and I waited to open our gifts, my mother played her Janet Jackson music as she and her boyfriend did their thing. By the time they finished, it was later than we had ever waited to open gifts. As I sat there watching my mother and her boyfriend lavish each other in jewelry and leather, I was given one box. When I opened the box, it was a red coat. Wow, all I got was a coat while they spoiled each other in matching garments. And to make matters worse, they got dressed and left me there to babysit with no working heat and we were not even allowed to watch TV in the living room.

I didn't respect her new boyfriend. Hey, I lost respect for any guy she brought around ever since the last guy she was in a serious relationship with tried to molest me and even tried to make it seem like he wasn't trying anything in the beginning. I remember him asking me if I wanted to go swimming, so I said yes and went to get my swimsuit on. When I got out of the bathroom, he was staring at my nine-year-old body like I was a piece of meat.

When my mom came home, she got on me for changing my clothes while she was not home. As a parent, that should have been the first sign he was going to try something else. Years later I came clean with her about everything after she told me he was locked up for actually raping a girl. It was pretty funny how he popped up later down the road, though.

As I sat in my cold house on Christmas night, I decided I was leaving. I now knew my mother and I would never get along and I had to tend for myself. So doing my winter break, I spent the night at my grandmother's house and used her cassette recorder. E. T. didn't try anything because he and I had stopped talking ever since the last time I kirked out on him. As I was there, I recorded my final good-byes on the tape as I counted down for Marsh to call and tell me he had gotten the place. I couldn't wait to be somewhere calm and clean with hot water and heat, somewhere that I could be a child and be free to have friends and concentrate on school. I couldn't wait until Marsh called me. I just wrote in my journal to help time pass.

> Dear Journal. Today is December 28. Sorry I didn't write in you. My Christmas was terrible. I got a coat. My mother paid more money on herself and her boyfriend than her own children. I don't like her boyfriend, and he better not tell me what to do. I will tell him about himself. My

mother spends more time with him than us. Not that that's not good for me. But it is messed up that I have to watch her kids Monday, Tuesday, and Yesterday.

Dear Journal. It is January 12. I hate my mother. She smacked me in the face. She will pay. I don't know how yet. Oh yeah, my mother and her boyfriend are supposed to be getting married.

Then Marsh got the apartment. Marsh and I had kept talking, but it was not until February that he told me about the apartment. I had already had my bags packed on the back porch for months. Whether it was Marsh's place or somewhere else, I was leaving soon. Now that I knew Marsh had the place, I had to figure out when it was time to leave.

The day had come for me to leave my mother's house for good, and once I left, I did not ever look back. I was fifteen years old, and my mom had been being very mean. She and her boyfriend were going through a breakup, and she was acting very evil. I had been stuck in the house every day watching my siblings, and we had no heat in our house for over five months. The whole winter the gas and heat were off, and we were forced to wrap in covers and boil water on an electric plug-in stove top to take a bath. My mom said she was going to pay the gas bill and told me to stay home. I begged her to allow me to go; I was cold and tired of being stuck babysitting. She threatened me to do as she said, and walked out.

As soon as she left, I knew this was my opportunity to leave, so I called Marsh to come get me. Marsh was trying to convince me to stay and work it out, but I knew there was no chance. Once Marsh arrived, I brought three large trash bags full of clothes to his car and two suitcases. I had packed my whole world. Marsh looked at me like I was crazy; he didn't know how serious I was until then. I put my siblings in the van and jumped in.

Everything was planned out from months before. I informed Marsh of my aunt's house where I was dropping off my siblings. Once we arrived, both my brother, who was two at the time, and my sister, who was eight, looked at me. I gave them both a hug and kiss. I ran to the side of my aunt's front door, and once I was sure that my siblings were in the apartment, I jumped in Marsh's van and he pulled off.

When we got to Marsh's apartment, I was shocked to see his babies' mother there. Marsh had not warned me. But once I was there, I started to take to her well. I didn't go to school for a week or so because I had just run away and I was trying not to be found. But later on, Marsh called my mom to let her know I was there. I begged my mom to allow me to stay, and since she knew I would run away again, she agreed. My mom contacted my new caseworker, and they gave Marsh temporary custody of me.

Everything was going great. Marsh was cool. He took me to school in the morning and even picked me up sometimes. I slept in the living room on the floor with pillows, and I even was able to talk on the phone with Mike. Marsh used to come in there and talk to me, and sometimes he fell asleep out in the living room too. Marsh's babies' mother didn't like it. She started getting jealous and wanted Marsh to send me back home. Hold up, I thought. When Marsh used to tell me what she would say, we agreed that I had agreed to move in before he even had a place; she was the one not supposed to be there.

As weeks passed, Marsh and his babies' mother started fussing more about all types of stuff. I just lay low, went to school, came home, and minded my business. I knew Marsh wanted her gone; he used to tell me all the time. He used to say he was only helping her out, and that they really were not together. He even said he thought one of the kids was not his. Marsh had other girlfriends he was talking to on the outside. I met one of them and was surprised to find out the girl was my age; Marsh was twenty-three. *Wow, men talking to young girls must be normal,* I thought to myself, *because everywhere I go, it's happening.* I just played my role not trying to make more confusion where I lived.

Marsh was not helping matters. One night as I got ready to sleep in the living room, he came out and started to flirt with me. "Oh no, not you too," I started to cry. Marsh pulled out twenty dollars I looked at him like he was crazy. I wanted to kick, yell, and scream, but I kept quiet: one, because I had nowhere to go, and two, I didn't want the mother of his children to find out what Marsh was trying. Again, I thought. I wanted no drama, just a stress-free life.

Days passed and Marsh was getting more bold and persistent, so on one particular day, I decided to prevent him from trying anything. I started to complain about my back hurting and lay in the bed with Marsh's babies' mother, with my head facing the opposite way. Marsh jumped in the bed and said he was sleeping in the bed too. Marsh's babies' mother looked at him and jumped up. Everyone couldn't fit in the bed, and she took her kids and lay on the floor. Marsh didn't budge. I begged him to move and let her sleep in the bed, but he said he wanted her to leave anyway. As night fell, I was asleep at one end, with Marsh sleeping at the other.

In the morning, his babies' mother packed all her clothes and left. I begged her to stay. I didn't want to be left alone with Marsh. It was only going to be a matter of time before he tried to make his move.

Chapter 14

Understand that people can't love others if they do not know how to love themselves. I appreciate people who know who they are so they know my value.

Once the babies' mother left, so did my youth. It didn't take Marsh long to try to take full advantage of me. I fought him off for months after she left, but it was getting harder; he was not letting up, and plus I never knew the emotions that Marsh triggered existed. I was determined not to allow him to share my soul, but what was the emotion and feeling going through my skin. I eventually gave into my curiosity, and a month later, I was pregnant. Marsh was twenty-three, and I was fifteen. He was my fourth cousin, whom I just met months before he had temporary custody of me and I was having his baby. Everything about this situation was wrong. Why me, why me? Again I dug deep within myself and started to write, and this is the poem I came up with.

Why Me?

Why me? Why does this stuff have to happen to me, why me? When I think I am running from one problem, I run into more. Why me? Why do I have to face so much when I'm so young, why me?

Why do I go through more than I can take? I wish I were a bird who could fly from this place or a frog who could leap from state to state. I wish I didn't have problems, you know. I wish my life were as simple as snow, but even though I know it can't be, why does everything have to happen to me? Why me?

Marsh and I had to keep it a secret, so the first couple months of my pregnancy were terrible. Marsh continued to date other girls, even sometimes bringing them to the house and introducing me as his cousin while he went in the room and had sex with them. I was sick to my stomach and cried many nights, "What have I gotten myself into now? Everywhere I go is a dead end." I started to become numb to the world, to life, and to people. I would cry myself to sleep.

As my pregnancy progressed, I was five months along and starting to show. It was time for me to go back to court. Marsh came to me and said he didn't want me to leave. I knew I was not in love with Marsh, but I wanted something different for my child; I wanted her to have both parents. Things started to take a turn for the worst when my family members found out I was pregnant and called the courts and told them I was pregnant by Marsh. My lawyer came to me and Marsh and explained to us that if I were pregnant by him, he was going to get locked up for statutory rape and I was going to be put in a home for pregnant girls, similar to a group home but worse. The group home experience I definitely did not want, especially with a baby. On top of that, I didn't want to be the cause for Marsh to go to jail. As my lawyer was explaining everything, I looked at her and said, "What can we do?" My lawyer informed me that there was not much. My lawyer then followed up by stating that if I and Marsh were married, the court would be forced to close the case.

So I went home and thought hard. We had only a few weeks left before my court date, and we had to think of something. After a few days, Marsh and I both agreed that getting married would be the best thing. Even though this was not what a traditional wedding looked like, it was going to save us both, and besides, my life was far from traditional. So Marsh and I both went to my mother and explained everything. We needed her signature at the court building because I was under eighteen, and where we lived, if you were fifteen and pregnant, with a parent's signature, you could get married.

As my mother sat back and listened to us and our situation, she agreed. I knew she didn't want to have to take care of me anyway, much less a baby, and besides, Marsh was stable. Just before she gave Marsh and me her final answer, she turned to Marsh and asked him for $300 to pay a bill and Marsh gave it to her. I felt like I was being sold to the highest bidder. Wow, $300.00 was my worth? So on October 23, 1994, Marsh and I got married.

A week later, we went to court. I had written the judge a long letter, but once the lawyer told him we were married, the case was closed and the judge didn't even see my letter. It went so fast. After eight years of being a ward of the court and having someone look over me, I was now being turned loose into the real world to live as an adult, and not even one month later, I turned sixteen.

Things got stranger by the minute once Marsh and I got married. He started acting like he didn't want me to go to school, and once word got out I was pregnant by him and not Derrick, things got even more confusing. Derrickwas trying to reach me, and I was ignoring him. I tried to call him months later and tell him I was raped and needed space. To my surprise, he was still being supportive and not trying to let go. Once I broke down and told him the truth, that I was pregnant by Marsh, he called me all types of names and refused to talk to me again.

A few months later, I stopped going to school, but before I stopped, I almost fought the girl that jumped me back when I lived in the group home. How ironic: the year I started high school, there Nita was walking in. Rumors around the school was she wanted revenge, but once it got back to me, my cousin and some friends damn near jumped her because I was pregnant—and later we found out that she was not talking about me but another girl. Once the other girl found out Nita had problems, that whole school year I didn't have time to worry about that: I had bigger problems. I was a wife and mother at sixteen, and not to mention I was soon to be a domestic violence victim.

Chapter 15

Dollars make more cents than love; love makes more bills than cents. Happiness makes everything, so let's go get it.

After my daughter was born, I didn't know how to bond with her. I was looking at this precious baby and was still confused with emotions. The relationship between Marsh and me was terrible. He had become more violent than my mother. With my mother, the courts were always watching her. With Marsh, I was an adult to the courts now, and my mom was nowhere around. The abuse with him got so violent at times; I could barely recognize parts of my body. I remember the time my face turned very red and what looked like freckles appearing all over my body within seconds, after he choked me so hard my body became limp and I passed out. I was only sixteen, with nowhere to go no one to call with a newborn baby.

Our arguments always stemmed from him getting caught talking on the phone in the middle of the night with other females. I remember waking up once around two o'clock in the morning and Marsh had gotten out of bed and gone to the bathroom. The door was locked, so I picked up the house phone and heard him on the line asking a female what she had on. I could tell the girl was young. I could hear Marsh making grunting noises and also sounds of whacking going back and forth. I started to cry and went and got the key to the bathroom. I charged into the bathroom just to find Marsh sitting in the tub masturbating. I screamed. I was so upset and hurt. Marsh jumped up and ran after me. He pulled me by the hair and started kicking me. He kicked me so hard my hip bone slipped and I fell to the floor.

I was stuck and could not move. "Stop, Marsh. I can't move," I screamed. He stopped after awhile and I lay there. About fifteen minutes later I tried to stand up, but I couldn't. It took me a week before I was able to walk again. I scooted all over the apartment floor. Marsh apologized for everything. But he wasn't sorry.

I soon realized he had a sex problem, and our phone bill was $2,000 from him calling sex lines. He even had a weird fantasy about me and him having sex in front of people while they watched. I remember one time we were driving downtown, and he stopped and tried to pay a bum to sit in the backseat and watch us have sex. I was too embarrassed to do it. I would just look at him like what was wrong with him, and I soon wondered if he was some kin to E. T. My image of men started to really be obstructed. I started to feel this was how the world and men were and things started to seem normal. I had nothing else to compare it to. So again I just did what I knew best: write.

Dear Journal,

Today is January 31, 1995. I had my baby January 26, 1995, at 9:23 a.m. She is now five days old, and she weighs six pounds. Marsh and I were fussing because a female called and I hung up on her. So he gave me the baby and then he bent my arm all the way back. I started to scream, and then he threw me in the chair, punched me in the arm, and dragged me on the floor, all because of this female. This was the second time. I have a cut on my arm.

Dear Journal,

Today is March 17,1996

After him dragging me on the floor,I was determined to leave one day; I just didn't know how or when. Marsh kept trying to pick fights with me. I remember him trying to play-wrestle me, and then it turned violent. He would start off like he was joking and then hit me real hard. One time he hit me and I walked away, stating, "I don't want to play." He kept pulling on me, and I pulled away. He got mad and pulled me by my hair. I had just gotten

fresh braids, so when he pulled my hair, the whole right
side of my hair came out from the roots and I was bladed
for a while.

Man, if only I had the strength of a man. I would have knocked him
out, and on top of that, I had no father or males to come and defend me.
I didn't get in contact with them until later down the road. My mother
would come visit us sometimes, and if she noticed a bruise, she would
ask, but she always played the middle person. As time started to pass, I
just started slipping deeper within myself until I completely shut down
to the world. My life for the next few years was very numb. Days, weeks,
and months, even years passed, and I didn't even realize it.

Again I turned to the one thing I knew—my journal—and I wrote.

Today is December 14, 1996.
Dear Journal,

I am depressed and sad. The guy I thought loved
me hurt my feelings. If I had known it was going to be
like this, I wonder if I would have fought to stay here.
Marsh still hits on me, and it really hurts. I don't want
to be with him anymore; I will just fake it until the time
comes for me to leave. I hope I run into a lot of money, so
I can buy a house and leave. It's just too much. I know I
will never be happy with him. Dear God in the name of
Jesus Christ, please help me in this situation. Help me to
be able to take on any challenge.

It wasn't until I started working when I turned nineteen that I started
to come out of my shell a little. By that time, I had already started
establishing credit, and my mind-set was focusing on getting out of
my marriage with Marsh. I had gotten pregnant twice after my first
child but had two abortions because I wanted no more kids with Marsh.
Marsh was so strict on me and tried to use manipulation on me so much.
I had dropped out of school and had never had a job until I turned
seventeen. He hated me working and would threaten not to take care of
the household needs if I worked. At first I was scared because I thought
I would be struggling like my mother, but after awhile, I learned I could

do the small things without his help. Sex with Marsh was cracking down. When we did have sex, we agreed to use the withdrawal method, since he refused to give me the insurance card and take me to my doctor for birth control.

In the summer of 1997, I was working at the mall when I started to get sick. Marsh and I had moved to an apartment located behind the mall. Marsh was offered a new job doing maintenance. I remember a week before we were supposed to move, we asked my mother if we could stay with her in her new apartment located three buildings down from where we were moving from. We needed to stay somewhere until our new apartment was ready. Marsh's parents said Marsh could stay, but their place was too small for all of us. My mother said no because she didn't get along with me. I was so hurt; she not only saw me to the streets, but also my baby. That's when I knew my mother and I would not ever be a real mother and daughter. It didn't help our situation when I tried to come to her even after that and ask her if we could have a relationship like most mothers and daughters; she just looked at me with a straight face and said, "No, you're married now."

It was also around this time that my mother took me and my daughter with her down to DC. I was sitting in the front seat, and we pulled up at a familiar place. We pulled up at the barbershop where my mother's ex-boyfriend worked—the same boyfriend who tried to rape me. I looked at my mother like she was crazy because I had eventually confessed to her about him molesting me. I was very confused why we were there. "Ma, what are we around here for?" I asked.

My mother's response was, "I am making him pay for what he did," and she went inside.

"Making him pay?" I mumbled. "The only way he could pay is go to jail."

After ten minutes of being in the car waiting for my mother's return, I started to rock my foot out of disbelief.

When she came out, she was putting money in her pocket, and he was walking out the door behind her. He walked to my side door and said, "Hello, Alex." I looked at him and rolled my eyes; I did not talk. He then stated, "You were always my favorite."

I could see my mom smile at him and ask, "Why was she your favorite?" in a curious tone. He looked at me and said nothing.

From that day forward, I never knew how to feel about my mother. Did she let this guy get away with what he did? When she got in the car, I asked her again, "Why did you bring me here?"

"I stated I was making him pay," was all she said.

I sat there confused. What the hell was making him pay? What did that mean? That has stayed in my heart and my memory to this day, and I promised myself to kill all hopes of ever allowing her back around. Just like my father—I only see them both as my earthly parents.

Things eventually worked out with the apartment complex, and they allowed us to move in early.

But later down the road, the same woman who refused to open her home for one week while my apartment got ready was knocking on my door two years later with no place to live with my siblings. And I opened my door.

While I was working at the mall, I had everything worked out. I made enough to pay day care and buy the things my daughter needed, but when I got sick while at work, I knew it had to be what I dreaded. I quickly took a test, and it was true: I was pregnant. I was so upset, but what had been a mistake quickly turned into my strength.

Again I turned to writing.

> Dear Journal,
> Today is Monday, February 08, 1996.
> I hate my life! I am pregnant again. I hate my marriage! Friday Marsh poured bleach on me and Listerine. So I left. When I came back in the house, I asked him for money for an abortion, and he started kicking me and hitting me. I hope I get a full-time position at my job. If so, I will work on my goals to leave him.

I was turning nineteen with my second child, and I also turned into survivor mode. This time it was not for me; it was for my children. It was one thing me going through this, but I refused to let my children live the same life. Marsh tried to convince me to quit my job. He made promises of doing more for me. He kept making points that I would not be able to afford to take care of two kids, and he promised not to help me pay for day care or anything else if I worked. That was when I realized he was trying to trap me yet again. Marsh was getting me pregnant to control me. Wow, women aren't the only ones that try to keep a person by having a kid. Marsh tried to get me pregnant so I would need and rely on him.

I paid Marsh's threats no mind; I had kids to take care of. Marsh didn't realize he was only teaching me how to live without him. So I prayed to God and came up with an idea. I did not ever want to depend on Marsh again, but I still had to take care of my kids and I couldn't afford to pay day care for two children. Especially like the day care my daughter was going to, where every day she came home hurt. That's when I decided to open my own day care. Yep, that was it; I was going to call it loving family child care.

I worked my butt off for the whole nine months of my pregnancy. I took day care courses and saved money. I starting buying everything my baby was going to need without relying on Marsh. I then went to a rental office and applied to rent a one-bedroom apartment where we lived to open up a day care in it. At this time, my credit score was high because while I was working at the mall, I started to apply for different credit cards, and once approved, I built my credit history by paying them off.

Marsh was getting jealous and even tried to fight me while I was pregnant. But he didn't know I'd had enough. All I can remember is us fussing and he pulled a knife out. My daughter jumped in and started kicking him and crying, "Get off my mommy." He bent over and pushed her away. That's when I took all my might and started to fight him, pregnant and all. I was not going to let him hurt my baby. The knife was still in his hand, and he grazed me on the back of my head. I began to bleed. I started crying, and for the first time, I picked up the phone and called the police. I went to the emergency room and received eight stitches in the back of my head. We ended up going to court, but I plead the fifth and used my marriage rights. That means the court could not force me to testify. After this situation I could feel my freedom coming soon. I just had no idea when. After that, Marsh didn't hit me anymore while we were still together. He actually started getting leery of me.

After I had my baby, I gave her a name to represent how the world was going to look at her. And from there, I started to fulfill her name. I was now going for all my Desires on earth. When my middle daughter was three months old, I opened up my first family child care, and my grandmother started to work for me. I was now on my road to success.

Marsh tried to do scare tactics, but I was numb. I had a mission, and it was to gain complete control over my life and to free myself from him and all the people that hurt me.

I didn't wait to go to the next level. A year later, I had saved over 10,000 dollars. I hired a driving instructor to teach me to drive, and I even bought a car. Marsh was mad, but I didn't stop there. I wanted a wedding, so I planned a church wedding in hopes that, I could finally have the fantasy wedding they played in my head, *may be me and Marsh needed a church wedding and things could get better*. Some of the many thoughts, which ran through my mind. But a day before the wedding, Marsh started to show his true colors and I was reminded of why I needed to focus only on me and my kids future, and not being someone bride. But it was too late to call off the wedding, I had already paid for everything and the guest were all lined up. So I and Marsh renewed our vows, but with no real emotions from me.

A couple months after that, I looked at my grandmother and told her, "I wanted a house for my kids." She looked at me and said, "If God put it in your heart that means you can accomplish it." So I quickly found a realtor, and we found a house. The house was seventy-two years old and very small, but it was going to be mine. Marsh refused to be a part of anything, and I was not mad because I knew it was only a matter of time before God gave me the okay to leave him, and I didn't want Marsh to have any claims on anything.

In the summer of 1999, I brought my first house all by myself. I was twenty-one years old. For months after buying the house, I used it only for business purposes and packed up and went to the apartment each day. But after a while of paying my mortgage and drifting even more away from Marsh, I soon moved all my things into the house and Marsh was packing an overnight bag to stay with me.

Things started going downhill in my marriage to Marsh, and it was completely gone. We had stopped having sex because I no longer was able to force my body to touch his. So I started to pray. To my surprise, I woke up one morning and had the strength of a thousand mules. I went to Marsh and told him I was not in love and needed a break. This was a year and a half after the purchase of the house and the renewal of our vows. Out of anger, Marsh insisted we take a month break; and from that point on, Marsh and I never connected again.

Our breakup destroyed Marsh. He started acting loco and even got so mad he gave up his parental rights. I was sad at first, but he was not a good dad anyway. So I accepted it. I tried to allow him to bond with my kids without me being around, but he refused. After years of my girls crying for him, I decided a person couldn't miss what he or she didn't have so I scratched Marsh out of our lives. But before I was able to scratch him, I was forced to move back to the apartment complex for a few months. That was a difficult time because it happened at the same time as Marsh and I separated. After the separation, Marsh started acting crazy and spying on me.

I had saved up some money and wanted to expand my house. I had totally renovated the seventy-two-year-old house before I moved in by replacing windows and doors, waterproofing, removing old trees, installing new carpet, painting, and even removing the oil tank and converting to gas. Even after all of that, the house was still too small. And my girls were getting bigger. So I hired my neighbor to add an addition, pave the driveway, replace the siding, and build a shed and fence. Once he was finished, I was so proud. His wife looked at me and said, "You should sell it." I was mad at her comment, I took it as an insult at first; I didn't do all that work just to sell it. I thought. But after careful thought, on top of Marsh starting to exhibit acts of a crazy possessed man, I knew moving was probably the best decision.. I put the house on the market, and within two weeks, I sold it for $140,000 dollars and I only owed $75,000. What an investment in less than two years! I had found a home around the corner, but God had better plans because the day we were supposed to go through closing, the whole deal fell through. I was devastated because I had to find somewhere where my business could still run, so I went back to the same apartment complex, rented another apartment, and did day care in it. This time I lived in the apartment. It was so hard to live there, but my loan officer had to work up a new deal and we had to find a new house. Marsh tried to torment me as much as he could. One day he came to my apartment and I came outside. He jumped in my face, and after that, I got a restraining order on him. When we went to court, he signed his rights over, and a month later, I found my new house.

I was twenty-three, and I had $30,000 in the bank from the sale of my first home $35,000 dollars from that sale had to pay off debts. I had to put down $20,000 because I was purchasing a brand-new three-bedroom house from a builder. I was proud of myself. The new house was about thirty minutes and twenty-five miles away from all my day care parents. I had three parents follow me, and after I bought furniture and household needs, I had $5,000 left in the bank. And only three kids in my day care. But everything worked out, and I became established in my new area. What once were three kids enrolled is now full and with a waiting list. Marsh was a thing of the past. My kids had not seen him since they were seven and ten, but they knew the story and were grateful for the truth. I knew I was going to leave Marsh and all my pain behind; I just never knew it was going to be at a time I still had my youth. I was proud of myself. I was finally able to stand up for me.

I later enrolled in broadcasting school trying to follow my dreams of being like my idol Oprah. I even interned at a couple places, but with my bills and the amount they started you off with in the broadcasting field, I couldn't take care of my family. I held a diploma in broadcasting, but I had to focus where the money was coming in at and that was day care. I tried other ventures, but everything led me back to day care. One exciting job I held along with running my business was my private investigator job. I was licensed and bore arms; I felt liberated and was starting to feel safe.

Chapter 16

Mesmerized by the eyes, analyzed by the unknown, completed not depleted by my life, and living to the fullest of my destiny.

Today is December 2, 2010, and it's been a long while since I wrote in you and a lot has changed. Two months ago, I suffered a miscarriage and am now on a path of trying again. Yesterday I found out Melton is married.

Even the girls are happy. Last night was a very meaningful time for them. They came back from the daddy-daughter dance with who I am starting to feel now is the man that is for me. I know you are wondering who? Just keep reading for the first time I can say that I am starting to feel a little complete. I am learning more and more that God knows what's for you and what's not, and he will place things in your life to remind you of it. This is a true testimony of that.

Well if you haven't figured it out by now, Robert and I is back together. Unlike other men my connection with Robert was not one which I was easily able to walk away from without me knowing we at least tried

Just two months ago I and Robert had a birthday bash with a couple of people from this group I formed. The purpose of the group was to gather women together as a sisters organization were we form love and support for each other. The group didn't last long after the birthday bash, but the birthday bash was a great turnout. Robert and I are also working on opening a business together, and I am continuing my education so I can expand my childcare business.

School is kicking my butt and life is very demanding, but it's great and I am happy for the most part. Thank you, Jesus, is what I say. I have been watching the Discovery channel, and the infomercials keep reminding me that Oprah is going to be off the air soon. So I am getting more eager to finish my book. I know with my life demands I will not be finished in time, but it is great motivation. Hopefully I will still meet her one day and share the details of my life.

It's like I still have more challenges and odds to overcome. Hopefully they will not be as horrifying as what I have already been through, but I know I need a little more fine-tuning before my story can be told. On that tip, Oprah, I will be there soon. It's funny; I rarely watch TV anymore and I never get to see Oprah's shows, but my love for her came from my childhood and seeing her as a hero who let me know I was a survivor.

The other day, I was at the hairdresser, and she turned to the Oprah show and the *Color Purple* reunion was on. I know you are probably wondering how I could be such a fan and not watch the show. My answer to that is because when I want something so bad, I hate to tease myself or remind myself of the accomplishments I have yet to achieve because it impacts me in the opposite way which is negative. I would rather work toward my goal blinded but knowing the path so at the end I can see without glasses.

After watching the *Color Purple* reunion, I saw how it has influenced my life. I was Cecily, I was Mrs. Sofia, and I felt like I was reuniting with the characters of my former self. I am sitting in the living room now thinking how happy I finally feel and praying and asking God for forgiveness for not praying and being as close to him as I usually am. I pray that this love with Robert lasts and that this time we make it happen. I pray that he becomes even more bonded with and believing of the Lord for the sake of our relationship, and I pray that we have a chance of getting pregnant and having a child the right way, with love.

Today is February 12, 2012, and a lot has changed. It's been over a year since I last wrote.

My grandmother passed this same month last year. I was blessed to become pregnant, and the baby is now five months old. Robert lost his mother just last month. With all these different life changes, I've turned to come back and write. I just bought a new computer, hoping to get over my writer's block. I wish I could let all my feelings and disappointments out without having to physically type. Typing can get annoying. It is like

I have so much to say, but my fingers can't move as fast as my mind full of expressions and thoughts.

I was told if you can write with both hands, then you use both sides of your brain. I guess that applies to me because my mind is always on overload. Even when I am sleeping, I am thinking. Yet again another tragedy has happened that has turned me within myself to write—on top of the fact I feel very alone. My relationship is not what I expected. I always thought that finding the one would be my key to happiness. But this is a new lesson in my life, and I am learning that happiness has always been with me; I have merely had to learn how to discover it within myself.

I guess I always thought with all the pain and suffering I endured as a child, I would one day have a knight in shining armor to come and rescue me. I finally gave that fantasy away with the fairy tales. I guess the life that is paved for me in this lifetime is me being the alpha to other people.

I am the person who is supposed to help others and teach them. I don't think there is anyone that is supposed to come into my life and rescue me but me and the Lord. The sooner I allow myself to stop depending on humans to make my life better, the faster I can stop putting people on pedestals and accept life for what it is, and maybe then—just maybe—I can start to enjoy life to the fullest and one day find real peace. But even then, I wonder if I will still have a still a sad feeling of being alone, especially when there are people around me who yet still do not take the time to really know me. I guess no one can really relate to me in my entirety of how I feel, so yet again I turn to the one thing that can understand me and that is —writing.

Today is February 19, 2012, and I am getting ready to go eat breakfast, but I just had to stop and type a little to get my fingers flowing and my brain open to all the explosive words that I need to write. My aunt passed last week two days before the one-year anniversary of my grandmother's death. It's crazy because both my aunt and my grandmother were very important to me in my childhood. They were the closest people to saviors on earth. Besides them, Grandma J, and my god mommy, there were very few people I could turn to protect me while growing up, and I have lost two of them in less than a year. But as I accept their deaths, I also learn so much more about their lives.

The thought of their deaths reminds me that I am on this journey called earth all alone, but now I am not scared. I have gathered enough life lessons and tools to protect me and my offspring along the way. My mother is supposed to be handling my aunt's services for tomorrow, with the memorial service being held at 11:00 a.m. at my aunt's church. I do not want to go for numerous reasons, primarily because the earthly family that God has placed me in is so unloving and dysfunctional. Even though I don't agree with my aunt for up and neglecting her family and especially me as years went past, I don't blame her. My aunt felt like this family never had her best interests at heart.

As I grow into a woman every day, I too can see her views and agree that the children my grandmother raised are all very off, starting from my mother. My relationship with my mother is very strained, and after losing my aunt and reflecting back on my grandmother's funeral and last years of life, I have come to the finalization that my mother is selfish and only cares about herself. As I write right now, the one lady that I cherished on earth is sitting in a storage bin surrounded by old furniture and teddy bears that my mother's lovers gave her. That's a terrible way to treat the remains of a woman you say you love. And yes, I know you are wondering what I have done to get her remains out. Well I did all I can do. I was the one who wanted her ashes and I remember the time my grandmother told me she just wanted to be free. I wanted to fulfill her last request and pour her ashes in the ocean and let her remains be at peace. As soon as I put my views in the situation my grandmother became a tug a war and I had no grounds because her children where the next of kin. As I sit here and think of my aunt and grandmother, a time comes up in my mind when my aunt showed me a sign of courage and protection. She was like my warrior princess. I can remember it like it was yesterday.

My aunt, my mother, and I were at my grandmother's house. I think I was about eleven years old. My mother was just being herself when she started picking on me. She starting saying hateful things to me, and all I can remember is her hand lifted up and a slap went across my face and knocked me down to the ground. My eyes pierced with anger, and I could feel rage run through my body. It's a good thing that even as a young child, I thought before I reacted. Scenes started to play before my mind, and seeing her dead was starting to look good right about that time.

As I literally picked my face up off the floor, I proceeded to run toward the front door. All I could hear was, "Bitch, get back here," as the anger started to pierce my spine. All I could think of was getting out; I ran out my grandmother's front door. But there was another door blocking me. You see, my grandmother lived in a duplex apartment building, with only four other apartments in her building. And there was a main door you needed a key to get out of. The rage was building, and so I threw my arm through the window of the door and broke the glass. I was so surprised at the rage, I started to scare myself. At that moment, I quickly pulled my arm back and saw that I was bleeding; the glass had sliced my wrist, going diagonally. It was a very deep cut. Once I saw the blood, I started screaming and crying.

My aunt ran out the door and quickly catered to my arm.

My mother started screaming, "Let her bleed to death, the dumb bitch."

My mother was still trying to attack me, so my aunt jumped in front and said, "I am taking this girl to the hospital. The glass split her wrist."

My mother kept yelling, "No, let her bleed to death."

My aunt looked at my mother and said, "You and I are going to fight if you don't get out of my way." My aunt grabbed my arm and we jumped in the car.

The doctor stitched me up. I had to get sixteen stitches. My vein had jumped when the glass cut me, I was cut right across the area where my main vein on my wrist was at. The doctor kept saying I was lucky because it was miraculous how my vein jumped and didn't get cut; if it had been cut, I would have bled to death on my way to the hospital.

Today is a bittersweet day; I am so tired of teaching people how to act. I just know I will teach my children the right ways of treating people.

I don't know why sometimes it has to take heartache, pain, or tragedy for some people to get it.

But I am learning that until I love myself fully, no one else will know how to love me either.

I was very standoffish in my preparations to going to the funeral, which was on Monday.

As I sat there in the church for the service, I kept thinking of when my time was coming.

When I thought of what I wanted people to remember about me, I wanted to be known for being loving, full of life, tough, ambitious, kind, giving, and most importantly, for loving God. Not to mention being a great mom and friend. With that being said, I turned my frowns to crowns and welcomed my family with my tender love.

After the funeral, we took my aunt's youngest son to dinner, along with his girlfriend and my other cousin and my brother. Everyone enjoyed themselves, and I felt good for the first time to be a part of my family. I learned I can't make my cousins suffer for the mistakes of our parents, but I can start a new tradition and make my family and children have what we didn't have growing up—a sense of worth and unity.

Today is February 23, 2012, and I am in a great mood. I woke up determined to lose weight and be healthy.

I want this summer to be my best. I started finding myself leaning toward my relationship as my happiness, but I was quickly reminded that I need to lean toward myself. My happiness will come once I am happy with me.

I graduate this year, and I am so excited I will receive a college degree. I will be the first in my family, of all my mother's and grandmother's children, to accomplish this, and I am proud.

My oldest daughter is being homeschooled, something I once did myself after I got pregnant with her. I have been homeschooling her for a year now. I refused to allow her to go to the neighborhood school, where she would be subjected to so much negative behavior. The school she was enrolled in disenrolled her due to boundaries. I recently started looking for more additional courses to add to her home school program.

As I searched the web, I came across a great program. My state is one of the few states that actually issues a high school diploma and not a GED. They also have an accelerated program for mature adults with life skills, who meet with a mentor weekly and show their life skills in order to receive their high school diploma. I was so excited to learn this, because even though I went to home school through the mail, I never felt it was a legitimate diploma and I never felt like it was accredited worldwide. So I signed up for the EDP course so I will have my diploma at the same time I receive my college degree.

I am so excited because even through all my adversities, I still stayed focused on my purpose. The day I stay still will be the day God will call me.

Once I receive my degree, my goal is to expand my day-care business. I have been building my business through business credit and locally so I can branch out very soon. I want to one day be able to offer my children a foundation and a purpose. Just looking at how my grandmother and aunt were buried with very few funds and no assets for their burial and even for their children, I am determined to leave my kids with the tools of survival. I want to grow my business up to become a larger corporation where my children are the presidents of the company when I pass. While I still have my youth, I must put this goal into effect.

Being around my family reminds me of where I came, jumping from house to house, being without electricity and boiling water on an electric stove at five o'clock in the morning just to take a warm bath before going to school. I was so scared of growing up and paying bills. And now to see my unstable mother living with my sister just motivates me even more to accomplish my goals.

Besides being an abused child, I was a poor child growing up. I hated my childhood and often hid in my brain, living in my thoughts and often poems to make my childhood go faster.

I mean I *really* hated my life. Just thinking of my childhood right now and allowing the wounds that I hid for so long to actually surface as I write is making me cry. I was extremely depressed as a child; there were times when I thought death was better. Not only did I not have a dad, but the two men that were supposed to be father figures—even my own cousin—tried to sexually abuse me,. On top of that, we lived in a home where I never felt stability, and my mother made me feel like she hated me for being born. I hated my appearance too: my buck teeth, my big lips, my stomach. Life was hard.

I remember writing a poem called "Suicide." It read like this:

Suicide

In the house by the lake, there I lay down and cry, running from my troubles, thinking of how to die. Could I hang from the ceiling, drown in the lake, stab myself with a knife, choke off something I ate?

Ten feet relaxing with the birds and the ants, having conversation, talking intimate chat. If I die today or tomorrow, will anyone care? Maybe I can die when no one is near. I wonder will my family care? They didn't when I was here. I just sit back and chill. Thinking of how to kill myself is a thrill. No one wants me anyway, so why should I be forced to stay? What if I jump off the building, dive in the pool, suffocate myself with a pillow, or eat poisonous food? Will I die fast or slow? I really don't want to know. Life is a trip, and that's no lie. I am getting tired of it; that's why I want to die. Maybe I should commit suicide.

After living this life and not knowing if there would ever be an end to my suffering, I am so happy about the strength and endurance God bestowed on me. I am more proud of the children that God has blessed me with and the strength they give me to do right by them.

I looked to my oldest daughter just today and told her she is my rock. She smiled with delight and said, "Wow, Mom, but I thought a woman's husband is supposed to be." I told her there can be many rocks, but she is the one that is the most solid.

Today is February 29, 2012. It is a rainy day. My weekend was a laid-back one. My aunt and I went to see the new Tyler Perry movie *Good Deeds*. I like Tyler and hope to be able to work with him one day. My aunt and I seem to be bonding, I guess because both of us lost someone who we were close to, my grandmother.

I guess that's how Robert feels about his sister even though they are not close. Robert lost his mother last month, and that was a very hard time for us. We were her caregivers, especially him. During the time of our mourning, I was forced to be around his sister, and it was very hard because prior to his mom passing, his sister and I had some words; after our conflict, I lost a lot of respect for her. But I put my feelings aside and extended my hand out on behalf of the love I have for Robert.

It is sad that Robert has now lost his mother. It was just two years ago that his mother and my grandmother were at Atlantic City. I know you're like, "What?"

Yes, Robert and I have overcome a lot, but in the end, he is the man who won my love and respect. It was hard to trust him after all he put me through when he was afraid. But after hearing his point of view and understanding his values, I was able to take a risk with my heart. And I am glad I did. One thing I love about Robert is his genuine heart. Unlike many relationships I had when the men had no real concern for me or my child, Robert comes off different. After really sitting back talking with him, I now understood Robert was afraid of not only hurting me but hurting my children as well if it didn't work. And after him dating a few women doing our breakup—all of whom had no children—he realized I was the one. I remember our conversation like it was yesterday.

We were at the park, and he said, *"Alex, I love you, and I don't ever want to feel the void I have in my heart without you anymore. I am scared to be a father of three, especially going from having no children, but my love for you is worth the risk. You have all the qualities I look for in a woman, and I am ready to learn how to be a father and a man to you."*

I was so surprised and scared to hear these words. I never gave someone a second chance to hurt my heart and this too was a learning experience, but like I mentioned earlier, this guy was different. It has been a year and a half now, and we live together building a future, with a six-month-old baby boy, and we are planning a ceremony soon. Wow, patience is a virtue.

Robert and I still have more growth to do, but we are doing it together. Even though I seem to have gained the love of my life, I am still not complete. I have much more to fix about myself, and it is mainly accepting and dealing with my past. After I attack all my past demons, I will be free to love without fear. So let's finish attacking those demons.

Chapter 17

I may not be where I want to be, but I am far from where I used to be.

This weekend, besides hanging with my aunt, I also decided to follow another dream of mine, and that is to look in to what it takes to open a boutique. I love to shop, and fashion is a pet pea of mine. I love antiques and finding old meaningful items from the past. For some odd reason it gives me a sense of purpose. Finding items that have been on this earth longer than me still lasting and bringing joy to someone else life now. That is what I want my life to represent. I want to bring purpose and joy even when I am no longer walking the world. Opening up a store where I could sell and store many pass memories is one of my next goals. As for now I know I cannot afford it. So I just dream of the time I would be able to. As I slept that night, God gave me an epiphany. I dreamed I owned a boutique at the shop around the corner from my home. When I awoke, I was so upset to find out it was just a dream.

Later that day, I had a taste for Subway, so I decided to drive down the street to the shopping center. Not even realizing that I had arrived next to the little boutique, were I purchase my body magic products once before. After I purchased my sandwich, I decided to go back in to the boutique to see what new products they had and to ask the owner questions about becoming a vendor. As I stepped into the shop, a positive feeling ran through my body, and I knew this was God talking to me. In just minutes, I was asking the owner about leasing options, and now I am about to lease a table in the shop to sell my line of products, which I will call Classy Creations.

As I sat there and chatted with the owner, we seemed to hit it off really good. Now I was on my next journey of fulfilling my dreams.

As I sit here and think of my life, I also want to give a tribute to my childhood friend, who is also a cousin to me, Tia Lynne Jackson, who passed February 9.

Tia was killed in a tractor-trailer incident. She was only twenty-eight years old, and she touched a lot of lives while she was here. Just by me looking her up on the web, I learned that she was a volunteer for young girls, a probation officer, and a co-owner of a store. Tia inspired me from just learning about her and all she touched in her short time.

My memories of her were from our earlier years, when she was only about five years old and I was like her big sister. We were five years apart. Even when she was younger, I remember her amazing smile and bright personality. Years after we disconnected, my mother would show me updated pictures of Tia. Her smiles always stood out. I wish I knew her as a woman. A part of her will stay in my fondest memories.

Tia and I parted paths around the start of all the pains of my childhood.

Today is April 6, 2012. Easter is in a couple of days. I have been in a depressed state ever since I had my baby; I put on some extra pounds that are hard to get off. And my insecurities have been kicking in a lot on top of that. Robert does not really make me feel sexy anymore, and our relationship can get a little monotonous. I don't really feel up to writing today so I will come back another time.

It's been about a month and a half now since I last wrote, and my hands feel so heavy from the words that have not been released weighing them down. I planned a trip to go camping, and it feels like a disaster. Robert has been complaining ever since we've been here. I sometimes feel like, what are we together for, I feel like everything I look for in a mate I still don't have, but I look at myself and everything I look for is in me. Like always, once people get comfortable with you, they show you their true self. I just sit back testing my level of tolerance, praying for things to get better with all I have endured, I don't have much patience. I am tired of teaching and so desperately want to be spoiled and treated like the queen I am.

As I am sitting here I get angry because Father's Day just passed and I am looking to see who I can give this Father's Day basket to.

As I start to think, I come up with my dad, and then I get angry all over again.

My father is no longer the drug-addicted crack smoker he used to be. He is now a college graduate with a stable job and a nice home, but he still is not here like he could be. But then I remind myself I really don't want to form a bond with him, because he will leave me again.

Growing up without a father was bittersweet. In some ways, it was acceptable due to the lifestyle he lived. And in other ways, it was not acceptable because a lot of the abuse I endured, especially from men, could have been avoided if I'd had a father in my life. When I was a little girl, men knew there was no father around me for them to answer to, and my mother was blinded to the truth, so men preyed upon me and my fatherless situation as they targeted in on me. Even if my father was around he couldn't be the type of man I needed. The type of man that fits the definition of a father, my definition of a father means that he knows there's a difference between protecting and preventing. He knows the transition from being someone who was selfish to one who is selfless. And he knows to be the first male that his daughter falls in love with, who teaches her about life. My dad has not ever filled these shoes.

I remember the time I was two years old and my dad gave me beer while we sat outside his mother's Southeast home in DC. I was running around and playing. It was a carefree time in my life. The second run-in with my dad was about eight years later. My mother and I caught the bus around his mother's way to visit. We walked to the clothing store in the area, and there was my dad hanging on the corner. I could tell he was not right in the head but he was functional, and he pulled me to the side and talked to me. I remember telling him I was not happy at home, but I didn't say too much because I sure didn't want to live with his drug-addicted behind. It was almost three years later when I saw him again, and he was worse off than before. He didn't even recognize me.

I was damn near twenty-two when our paths met the fourth time; it was because of my determination to find out the truth that it even happened. In my whole life up until the age of twenty-two, I had only seen my father three times since birth. It was not really planned how it happened. One day my cousin reached out to me and called; her name is Melody. Melody and I were so close when we were small. Our fathers were brothers, and my mom dated both of them. Melody saw me at the bus stop and recognized my face; we later communicated from time to time. Melody told me she had my Uncle Ray's number, so I called him and he gave me the 411 on my father. He let me know my father was incarcerated in one of the detention centers in Virginia. I then called around until I found the one he was in, got his inmate number, and wrote him.

I couldn't allow Marsh to know I was writing him. He would get upset if he knew another man was around, even if he were my father. So when I received the first letter and the others that followed, I hid them. Writing my father actually gave me the strength to stand up to Marsh. I guess in some weird way, Marsh was a father figure to me up until then, he demonstrated the qualities of a father figure: *an older man, often one in a position of power or influence, who elicits the emotions usually reserved for a father.* When I received the first letter it read:

> Hello, Alex. 11:42 3/6/99
>
> I hope this letter arrives to find you and family in good spirits. As for me, I am fine and truly have been blessed with another day of life and by being granted that I am able to say: I love you! Don't worry; I will never stop writing you. First, let me inform you that I never knew all the things you went through as a child were so serious. As I read your letters, I feel guilty for not being there for my dream baby. I wanted and dreamed of a daughter like yourself, so beautiful and precious. I just was not in the right mind-set to be able to love and treat you the way you deserved. Alex, I can sense by the tone of your letters there are forces keeping you back. I totally understand your position and hope you are able to not allow those forces to keep you from growing. Alex, thanks for being so inspiring to me. Knowing that my daughter is open to learning about me gives me strength to do what I have to do once I am released from these prison walls.

After reading this letter, I wondered how he could say he loved me when he didn't even know me. I just couldn't understand. But as we bonded, I saw things about my father that were like me. He was smart. He was intelligent, and he was very artistic. That's when I was able to understand where I got my characteristics from—the kind heart, the big lips, the deep nature. And even if I never spoke to him again, I was fine; I learned something new about me.

Four months later and over six letters from the both of us, he was released from jail, and we were able to turn our writing to phone conversations. I even bought him an outfit and had it delivered to the jail so he could have a clean, fresh outfit to wear home. I didn't do this because of love for a father but because of love for myself. I wanted the man who helped put me on this earth to have pride. And I knew small steps of encouragement would lead him on a positive path.

We continued to talk, and I later met my younger siblings, one of whom was the daughter of the lady that lived in the crack home I visited when I was young. I later found out her mother died, and she too was a ward of the courts. I took my sibling under my wing; she was twelve years old at the time. I showered her with love and showed her what a sister and a healthy lifestyle look like. At this time, Marsh and I were no longer together. I always warned my half-sister of drugs and how her chances of becoming an addict were higher because she was conceived while both her parents were drug addicts. We grew to know and have love for each other. She even graduated from high school with a 4.0 grade-point average and had colleges sending her scholarships, but once she turned nineteen, she ran wild and started doing drugs after being around the wrong crowd. We eventually broke apart. I immediately felt like I had failed her, but I later realized I did all I could do. The last I heard, she had a child and was on the system and trying to clean herself up.

While I was bonding with my half-sister, my father stayed in contact with me. I always kept him at a distance, mainly because I was afraid of losing him again. He had turned his life around and was doing good, but his past had caught up with him and he was living with HIV. My Sister mother died from this same disease years prior. HIV stands for human immunodeficiency virus, which is a lentivirus (slowly replicating retrovirus) that causes acquired immunodeficiency syndrome (AIDS), a condition in humans in which progressive failure of the immune system allows life-threatening opportunistic infections and cancers to thrive. Infection with HIV occurs by the transfer of blood, semen, vaginal fluid, pre-ejaculate, or breast milk. Within these bodily fluids, HIV is present as both free virus particles and virus within infected immune cells. I googled information, and that is what I got thanks to http://en.wikipedia. org/wiki/HIV. I really refused to form another attachment, not because he is living with this disease, but I grew up longing for a father and I don't ever want to long for him again—and then lose him.

So I have chosen to love him at a distance. I know one day he will leave or be taken away from me again. A tear flows down my eye because, being a Christian woman, I don't want to hold anger or fear in, but with the life I have been living, in order for me to protect myself, it seems like I have to.

Writing this reminds me of the time I finally met his mother after not seeing her since I was very young. My mother had come and picked me up from my other grandmother's house; I was living with her at the time because I had changed the grades on my report card. I messed up the report card so bad you couldn't tell what the grade was, and I had no other choice but to tell on myself. My mother didn't want the courts to have another incident on file, so she called my grandmother to come get me before she lost her cool.

Once my mother picked me up, she took me over to the house of my father's mother. I had to be like ten years old at the time. I was so excited to finally see her because everyone said I looked like her. When I walked in the door, she smiled so bright and hugged me. She was a very round lady with hips and butt; she had light eyes and very light skin. I had finally seen whom I resembled. It was a nice reunion.

A couple weeks later, I was eating dinner with my other grandma and the news was on. A shocking update came on the television: they were broadcasting that a lady died in the waiting room of a DC hospital. I looked up curious of what had happened to this poor lady, and there she was: the name and picture of my dear grandma. I searched the web about her death in the waiting room, and this is what I found:

Family Says Woman Died Waiting for Hospital Help
OTHER NEWS TO NOTE, WASHINGTON

April 16, 1990

A 63-year-old woman collapsed and died in a waiting area at D.C. after being all but ignored by hospital staff members, relatives say. "No hospital personnel ever touched my mother, not until after she was dead,'" Mariah

Evans told The Post. Martha Jackson waited about three
hours for treatment after walking into the emergency
room Monday night with several family members. She
had complained of chest pains and shortness of breath,
Evans said Thursday. During the wait, Jackson said
she was feeling faint, Evans said. Evans' sister went
for help, and others in the waiting room began yelling.
"Finally someone came out," Evans said. "But she just
stood there looking at my mother." Jackson was taken
into the emergency room a short time later after family
members and others placed her on a gurney. David
Heard, the hospital executive director, said in a statement
that officials are investigating Jackson's death, which
was attributed to a blood clot in her lungs. David Heard
declined further comment.

Imagine feeling happy to see her and looking forward to more times,
and then actually learn about her death while eating dinner. I jumped up
from the dinner table and cried. I fell to my knees and shook my head.
"No, Grandma," I screamed. "I just saw you." As time passed, I later
accepted that God allowed me to see her one last time before her death.
He wanted me to see the smile I inherited and to meet the woman who
carried a similar heart as mine. Her children later sued the hospital, and
they settled. The hospital is no longer open.

As I write this, I sit here and cry. I have been through so much, and
I pray God doesn't let my pain be in vain. My strength comes from the
reward of success that I fight to achieve.

I wrote the following poem when I was ten about both my parents:

Unforgiving Love

Unforgiving love is a love you will feel such as a mother
who beats on her child. Unforgiving love is a father who
left without a care, and didn't even look back and share.
Unforgiving love is sad because I feel this way about my
mom and dad. And why is the question some may ask.

I say if you know and feel what I feel, you will have unforgiving love as well. One that feels this way is truly hurt. I myself have unforgiving love, and as time grows, God will show me the way to forgive and spread love every day. To forgive is to forget, but to remember is unforgiving.

Chapter 18

Fantasize how one moment can change a lifetime, one second can predict your path, one thought can change your vision, and one decision can alter your plans.

One more demon to tackle; here we go. I was at least fortunate enough to have my father be able to stand up for me with this situation. I can honestly say I stood face-to-face with the devil himself. This person tried to turn my world upside down. If I knew then what I now know, I would have slapped myself to reality. I was so happy to close the chapter of this person. From the time this person entered my life, I had demons all around me.

His name was Tim. I met him right after I broke up with my older son's dad in 2005. We hit it off fast. I was rebounding and also was going through the stage women go through after having a baby. My older son's dad was younger than me, and he was not ready for a baby. I didn't want to repeat any cycles, so I let him go. I wished I knew that before I went through with the pregnancy. I would have waited to have my son, but the love I have for him in my heart is unconditional. So he was meant to be here.

It was a spring month, and my best friend at the time and I had agreed to go out that night. Once we met up, she told me of this club that was near the waterfront that these two girls we both knew from school's brother worked at. They said he could get us in for free. At the time, I was actually excited to go out and was looking forward to having some fun. Once we arrived at the spot, it was crowded. I think there was a special event going on, and the place was packed. As I was standing there minding my own business, this guy kept eyeing me down. I started rolling my eyes. If I had known all I was running into, I would not even have gone to the club. While standing there conversing with my friend I look to my left and there he was standing right beside me. Damn I thought this guy was determined. As he started to talk I also realize that he had swag like no other. Huh I thought he also don't know what he was getting his self into. If only I had a psychic with a crystal ball in front of me tell me my future. I later found out he was a con artist, robber, and womanizer. To top that off, he was my soon-to-be-husband. Where's the exit sign when you need one?

Carolyn and I walked over to the bar and ordered a drink. Being an amateur drinker, I didn't know what to order. I didn't drink or club too much, so I was gaining a new side to life. Before my son's father, I had not been with anyone really other than Marsh, and we never drank. His sense of fun was going out playing with the neighborhood kids or playing hide-and-seek, which was rather odd for a grown man. So as you can see, drinking was new to me. As Carolyn and I were standing there, the bartender took our order. I ordered an apple martini. And from the time I had drunk that drink the was the moment that started the beginning of the unhealthiest adult year of my life.

As I was sipping on my apple martini, Tim walked over to where I was standing. He started to whisper in my ear all types of things. As I was standing there, Carolyn turned to me and whispered, "That's their brother." I thought to myself, *then he must be half way decent.* I didn't find out the story of Tim until I was in too deep. After hearing what I thought was confirmation that he was a good guy from my friend, I began to loosen up. As the night went on, things were starting to become fun, and the drinks started to kick in. Before you knew it, we started to dance, and our bodies were in sync with each other. I thought, *this guy is actually able to keep up with me on the dance floor.* Before the end of the night, the chemistry was very strong and we exchanged numbers.

After a couple days passed, he ended up giving me a phone call. This guy was smooth. We went out on a date, and he wanted to be around me all the time. I had no clue he was living with a woman—or that he'd been locked up. I was in for a treat. Tim started to come around all the time, and at the time it was fine. He kept me company and helped me get my mind off my breakup. As time went on, I started liking Tim, but something was mysterious about him. I just couldn't put my finger on it. Then weird things started happening.

We had been dating for a few weeks, and one of my must-haves is to check out the place that the man I am dating lives. I told Tim that in order for me to take him serious, I needed to see where and how he lived. This secretly helped me know if he were a clean person and if he lived with a woman. Everyone can tell a woman's décor choices. I'm not saying men can't decorate, but women just have a little different flair. So one day as we were driving to dinner, Tim pointed to the complex where he lived. I looked at him and said, "Take me to your place."

Tim looked at me and said, "Al right, man, since you keep pressing me about it, I will take you."

We pulled up at his apartment building. He lived on the total opposite side of town in a neighborhood that was not bad, but I still would not feel comfortable leaving my vehicle at night if we grew to that point.

Tim quickly jumped out of the car. He looked at me and said, "Stay here." He then looked back at me again and said, "I must make sure that the house is clean."

As he was going to the apartment, I just sat in the car and observed the area a little more.

Tim quickly came back outside and reached for my hand. He looked at me and said, "Come on, baby. Let me show you my place."

As I walked in the hallways, I felt a little nervous. When I walked into the apartment, it was decorated beautifully. That's when I started to realize either this was not his house or he lived with a woman. Tim showed me all around the apartment. except one room. I looked at him and said.

"Tim, let me see your bedroom,". The door to the bedroom was closed. Tim quickly stated that the bedroom had water damage and it was not safe. I had no reason to doubt his response, but I just knew I would later have to see it if we were going to develop trust.

After leaving his apartment, I felt a little more trusting of him. I mean, what man brings you to a home he shares with another woman, knowing you can pop up at his place anytime? Right.

Time went along, and the many demons of Tim started to unfold a month later. He started wanting to be around me even more. Things were moving fast, and I wanted to get confirmation from God if this was what he wanted me to do. So I started praying to God that if this were not where he wanted me to be, to remove this guy.

Three days after I put that prayer in the universe, Tim had left my house one night and the next day, I received a phone call. The voice on the other end was Tim's children's mom calling to tell me Tim was locked up. Was this god warning? I talked to his children's mother briefly, and just when I hung up the phone it rang again.

"Hello," the voice said. "Is this Alexandria?"

"Yes," I replied, "but how do you know me?" I had no clue who she was.

"My name is Brenda," she replied in her strong Island accent. "I am the lady Tim lives with."

I didn't say much; I just stood there with the phone in my hand in shock. I started to think, if he lives with her, how is that possible when he's always with me?

I soon learned Tim did live with a woman and she was in the room when I came to visit. "Do you have a red car?" she asked me.

"Yes," I replied.

"Wow, he told me you were his cousin and you had to use the bathroom. He asked me not to come out of the room." She then added he had no car and she was paying all his rental car bills. She started to go deeper in the conversation and added how violent, abusive, and evil he was.

I was in shock. What man brings his new girlfriend to the same house with his current girlfriend and neither one knows the other is there? Either this was not true or this guy was damn good. All types of things were running through my head. I started to think if he was all that bad, then why was she still with him and why was she still paying his rental car bill? I wanted to talk to Tim to find out why he disrespected me by bringing me to his and his girlfriend's home. I quickly ended the conversation because I had no clue what her motive was. And I needed to clear my mind.

Moments after I hung the phone up, Tim's children's mother called me again. Tim had contacted her and asked her to call me. As we talked, I quickly asked her who Brenda was. She started saying a crazy older woman who was obsessive over him.

Days passed, and it felt like weeks. Anxiety was building in me, and I needed answers. All these women were calling me one was saying negative things about him, but that was not the guy I saw, and if he was so bad, why was she still around?

After four days, the moment had come: Tim contacted me. I listened, and he explained. He stated he and Brenda lived together but he was trying to get her to depart before I found out. He stated he gave her a thirty-day notice. He also stated once he started dating me, he knew he had to make her leave; he said he wanted to impress me and didn't want to lose me, so he took a chance and brought me to his house. He also said how it was almost close to her leaving and then he was arrested.

I was confused. I also felt special in a weird way. If this were true, this guy must really like me in order to go through all that, right?

Weeks passed, and Tim was still locked up. He had two warrants out on him, each for $100,000. Tim was being charged with false imprisonment, assault-first degree, armed robbery, and con-armed robbery. Things just didn't add up. After I further investigated, I learned one of the charges against him was when we were together at the time of the incident. The allegation was that Tim and two other guys robbed a hotel and had guns. I knew this was not right because we were at the movies at the time of the event. After seeing and knowing this was a false allegation.

I then wanted to learn more about this lady who had called. So when she called me back, I took the call and listened. Off the top, she quickly warned me of Tim and how she was going to use this opportunity to move away. She explained to me that once she noticed him not ever coming home, she called the phone company and asked for a detailed bill. She said she saw my number and even checked his voice-mail messages and heard my voice. She said she and Tim started arguing more over me, and she knew he was falling for me.

I sat on the line listening to this woman, trying to put the puzzles together, trying to figure out this guy. He just didn't seem like the monster she was painting. I mean, he treated me very well. I never spent money, and he was very attentive to my needs. So who was she describing? I started thinking she was a woman scorned and hurt that her young boyfriend was falling for someone else. I also put two and two together. She was the anonymous caller that got Tim arrested, all because he fell for me. So from there, I was determined to help him get home. I always kept what she said in the back of my mind just in case some parts were true. Then I began my mission of getting him home.

Looking for clues and solving the mystery started becoming adventurous; it worked my investigative skills and I was learning court terminology and more about how the system works. After a few weeks I had learned the ins and outs of the system. When Tim called me, I always had new information for him and new things and steps to better his case. Three months passed, and Tim and I talked about marriage. I was not sure if it was going to work or if he truly had a dark side. But for some odd reason helping Tim was adventurous, so I gave him the benefit of the doubt. I thought maybe he had not found the right woman until now, and that's why he had hurt the other lady. I was a strong believer that men are dogs until they find the woman that sweeps away their heart. I felt Tim looked at me that way.

So I got everything prepared on the outside. I got a prenuptial agreement written up stating all that I acquired before the marriage was mine. I had to protect myself, just in case. I dressed up in a suit and went to the jail. He signed the prenuptial agreement, the notary there stamped it, and we said I do. Again my marriage was not a traditional wedding. A month later, we went to court because it looked good in the court's eyes if he had a family. The state attorney had no proof, and the three main charges were dropped. Tim and I were happy, but he was still being held on one charge and the bail was lowered to $20,000. I cried as I walked away, knowing there was no way I could help him. But I went back and did more research and later found out that the judge had set the bail for 5 percent to be paid.

Tim called, and we talked about everything. He told me he had a stash of money put away at his mother's house, and if I could just come up with the money, as soon as he got home, he was going to give it to me. Me and Tim parents did not have any relationship they still wanted Tim to be with his children's mother so again I made him sign another document and notarize it. This time it was a promissory note stating he would repay me. I found a bail bondsman and charged my credit card. Tim had no clue if I was going to truly go through with it, but I prayed that God would get me out of this situation if I were blinded, so I went to the jail and picked him up.

When Tim walked out the double doors, he ran and picked me up. We both smiled and gazed in each other's eyes; it was like a movie scene. When we arrived home, we just laid beside each other without being intimate; I guess we were still in shock.

After a month of Tim being home, everything was perfect. We did everything together. I later came to him and told him he needed to get a job. If we were going to stay together, I was not taking care of any man. Tim quickly came to me and said he found a job, so for two weeks, he went to work, and when it was time to pay, he came to me with a written letter saying that the company was holding his check. I looked at Tim, but he promised to fix the situation; he quit that job and started to look for a new one. And he found it. He started telling me that he was going to get a raise after ninety days at the new job, and every time he got paid, he gave me the check. Things were moving smoothly; they were working out.

After two months of him being home, changes came. I found out I was pregnant and Tim was happy, but for some odd reason, I was not. I despised my pregnancy and felt no bond with the unborn fetus. It was unlike my other children, where I felt connected. This pregnancy, I felt rage and hate; I felt like someone was taking over my soul. Tim started acting cocky and very demanding. Flashbacks of my conversation with Brenda ran through my head. Tim was starting to leave the house more, and things did not add up. I began to feel like I had just opened my life to the devil.

As the weird things started unraveling, I went to Tim's children's mother for answers; she knew more about him than I did. So on one Saturday morning while Tim was on a so called job seminar I called her and she confided in me that he was abusive, she also stated she was happy that he was with me now so she could have freedom. She explained that Tim was controlling and have beat her up numerous of times, I also found out that Tim never held a job until he met me. And the job he claimed he had when we first meet was not real and his badge was fake too. I asked her about the job he first got when he came home where the company was holding the check. She told me she wrote that letter and gave him a fake pay stub because he told her that his probation officer needed proof of a job she also let me know Tim stayed at her house every day doing that time, while faking on the phone with me like he was at work.

"Wow, he lied to me," I replied. Tim was really at his kids' mom's house chilling and calling me saying he was at work. This guy lied so much, he was a true con artist. He was so convincing. Who really goes to the levels he went through to prove his lie? It was so bad, he was so convincing, if you had on a blue shirt, he would make you think it's red.

She also told me Tim had her think he was using women to better their relationship, but once he got with me and married me, she started to realize she was the one being used. She told me about his first baby's mother and how she heard she skipped town with Tim's son because of how abusive he was. She then asked me if I owned a ring and some jewelry, and she described the ring and jewelry pieces. I ran to my jewelry box, and my pieces were gone. Tim had stolen my jewelry. I was in total shock. I asked her why she had never warned me before. She said Tim threatened her if she ran her mouth, and she then begged me not to tell.

I sat there, shocked again, wondering what I was going to do and how I was going to get this guy out of my life and out of my house without a fight. All this time I had thought Brenda was an obsessed woman, and part of that was still true; she even wrote Tim in jail a couple of times stating she loved him—he showed me the letters. At the end of the day, her story had substance to it, and to make matters worse, we had a trip planned to go to Florida and a cruise coming up.

I had to play everything out safely. If he was abusive like they said, I had to think with my head and not my heart. I didn't want him to beat on his babies' mother or try to fight me once he knew I found out. I had enough of fighting. The next move I was going to make to anyone that struck me was death. I had to come up with a plan and quickly. First, I had to stop the pregnancy. I was not too far along, and I had heard of the pill. So the next day I called my sister and I asked her to take me to the clinic. On my way to the clinic, we stopped at the community hospital. There I used their phone and called Tim. I wanted him to have the hospital number on his phone in case he started doubting my story. I told him I was having complications and was going to the doctor. Once I hung up the phone, we left and went to the clinic. I paid for the pill and took the first one in the office. The doctor instructed me to take the second pill the next day. He stated that the second pill would start the bleeding.

So that night, I faked cramps and twisted my body in the fetal position. I didn't and still don't promote abortion, but I do promote not being stupid. Tim looked upset. He too had thought getting me pregnant was going to trap me, but I was two steps ahead of him. The next day, the bleeding started. It was hard staying in the house with a liar and thief, and now the trip was coming up.

While I was pregnant, Tim also started showing me signs he was talking to another female. I had checked his phone and saw naked pictures of a woman's body parts. All this I keep bottled up until we went on our trip. I wanted to let everything out, but I just had to do it smart. In case he tried to fight me, I wanted it to be away from my business and away from my children. I refused to jeopardize my kids and what they saw or my business. So I just kept everything in until we were away. But my plan was in order.

During this time in my life, I started having dreams and feelings of darkness around me. One time I fell asleep, and when I woke up, I couldn't move my body. I could see my daughter at the bottom of my bed watching TV, but I couldn't talk or move; it was like I lost total control of my body. I started to pray and say *"rebuke Satan in the name of Jesus Christ"*, and the trance was lifted. I called my girls and told them if they noticed me asleep to shake me. I tried to stay awake as long as I could. Later I was told that the devil was trying to gain my soul and that was what you call spiritual warfare—where God and the devil were fighting over you.

I then started having dreams. These dreams were not ordinary. I saw my grandfather. I remember asking my grandfather why he was there because he was dead. And he replied, "I am dead, but I will always protect you." I woke up and was in shock, I was sweating so much. The dream was so real. Before my dream the last time, I had contact with my grandfather I was ten. The shortly after that he died. It was kind of funny, but my grandfather and I had an unspoken bond like no other. We never said we loved each other, but I knew he loved me by the way he looked at me or gave me his favorite cookies, Fig Newtons, every time I went to visit. My grandfather was a professional boxer in my area, and I always felt protected being around him. So when he died, I took it a little hard. After I had that dream I knew my Grandfather was telling me he was fighting those Demons that wanted my soul and he was going knock them out.

Before his death, I had never experienced death in my family. I remember staying up all night writing a poem for his funeral. It read:

> *The death of my grandfather was a hard hit; it makes me sad just to think about it. The loved ones he left were sad and blue. My Aunt and uncles cried. How about you? Yes, my grandfather is gone, and it's hard to believe someone can*

leave this family. I know it was time for him to go because God and his spirit said so. Even though he has gone away, he will be with me every day. The death of my grandfather makes me cry; just thinking about it makes a tear fall from my eye. He wasn't a perfect man, but he was always willing to lend a hand. I love my grandfather, believe I do, and if you knew him, you would too. I know he has gone away, but his spirit is with me every day.

Chapter 19

Emotion is deeper than a bottomless pit; you have to stay on top or you will keep falling.

When you marry the wrong person, it could mess up your life.

After my grandfather came to me in my dream, I knew I could tackle Tim. Once we got to Florida, we arrived at Ft. Lauderdale. Tim was still telling more lies, but everything had been revealed and the wool over my eyes was lifted. Tim continued to text on his phone. He told me the lady at his job, which supposedly was his so-called assistant, needed him. I looked at him like he was crazy. His lies were becoming more impulsive.

Later that night, we went outside the hotel for a walk. Tim's phone rang, and it was again his so-called assistant. He ignored the phone call, and that was my opportunity to dive in. I started off by asking Tim about the pictures in his phone. Tim's response was that he found a memory card with pictures at work and kept them. I looked at him, and shook my head we then started fussing. <u>One thing I hate is a liar.</u>

I turned away from Tim and started to walk back to the hotel. He started pulling my clothes, trying to convince me that what he was saying was true. I just ignored him, pulling away. Tim got furious and threw my keys in the street. I walked to the hotel even faster. His violent side was starting to show, but this was not the time or the place, not just yet.

The next day we went on the cruise. We barely talked. I was stewing inside and was waiting for the moment to let it all out. While on the cruise, we sailed to the Bahamas. I was able to see the native people, and I even purchased some souvenirs. The Bahamas was a very poor country at that time. As we wrapped up in the Bahamas, we were back aboard the ship. The sail back was rough for me; I started getting motion sickness and passed out. Tim told the paramedics on the ship I had just suffered a miscarriage and my body was trying to heal.

Once we arrived back to Florida, we had a four-hour drive to Orlando, our third and last destination on this so-called vacation. The room in Orlando was beautiful, and I was saddened that I was not in a position to enjoy it. Tim went into the bathroom and got on his phone. I knew now was the time to let it all out. He came out of the bathroom and fell asleep.

I knew I needed more proof to back up my argument; I couldn't tell him what I really knew because his kids' mother was at danger. I looked through his phone, and there was the proof. He had a text in his phone stating, "Why you not texting me or calling me back? Is it your wife again?" Rage and reality all hit at once. Not only was this man a liar and a thief; he also was trying to do me the same way he did Brenda. But I was not going to allow myself to be broken and disoriented over any man.

I quickly woke him up and started to pack my bags. "I am done," I screamed. "You are a liar and a cheat, and I refuse to be like your ex."

Tim cleared his eyes, jumped up, grabbed me, and said, "What are you talking about?"

I bent over, picked up his phone, and said, "This."

He took his phone and saw the text. Rage built in his eyes, and he was furious. He started walking toward me, and I started to look to see what I could throw. The lamp beside me was looking real good. But then I thought of my children and my house and all I had to live for, and I ran out the door screaming for help. Tim chased me down the hotel hallway. He grabbed me by my arm and started to pull me back in the room. Once I arrived in the room, he demanded I sit down or he was going to hurt me.

I yelled, "Hell, no," and ran out the door again. I ran so fast until I was out to the front desk. I asked the front desk to call the police.

Once the police arrived, I told them the story, and they escorted me back to the room to get my belongings. When we arrived, Tim was in bed watching TV. "Oh, you back to work this out?" he said. No, and the police told him he had to leave the premises. He grew madder and started to be hostile to the police. The police again gave him a warning and told him since his name was not on the room, he could not stay.

I grabbed my bags. But I could not find my purse. Tim had hid it.

I guess he knew once I left the room I was going to return because the keys and my ID and credit cards were all in there. "He hid my purse," I told the police. Tim denied that, and the police couldn't search him. So I grabbed everything I had and left. Good thing I had my truck keys in my suitcase for when I arrived back home.

The hotel staff was nice. They placed me in another room and kept it anonymous. Tim had only thirty minutes to pack and leave, and the manager had to stand in the room while he packed his things. I let the manager know he had my purse with the rental car keys in it, and the manager informed him that if he were caught driving the car, he was going to get locked up. He quickly gave the manager the key.

As I sat in the anonymous hotel room, I started thinking what I had to do next. I knew once we got home, it was not over. Tim rang my phone for three hours straight, but I would not answer the phone. He had his mother call me and even his children's mother, but I refused to answer. I needed to get my thoughts together, and then he finally left a message.

He said, "Sorry, babe. Please answer the phone. I cannot stay on the premises. The manager said I have to leave. I been walking around outside, I have nowhere to go, so if I don't hear from you soon, I am taking a shuttle back to the airport. And then I am taking a plane back home."

Damn, he had my credit cards and ID. I quickly called my credit card company and canceled my cards. But he must have left the message earlier and I was just getting it because he had already charged my card at the airport. I then told them I was stuck in Florida and I needed them to rush me my card there. They told me they could overnight the card, but I was going to get it late the next day. Wow, I was stuck in Florida with only fifty dollars to my name.

I went to the front desk and let them know my card was being rushed there and to let me know once it arrived. The manager handed me the rental car keys. I took the keys and drove around Florida, and I actually felt peace. I took myself to an all-you-can-eat restaurant and even enjoyed the alone time. Once my card arrived the next day, I decided to finish the days of my trip there alone. I shopped and started to prepared myself for the big event I was about to face once I arrived home.

Tim continued to call me but I refused to answer the phone when he arrived at the airport all my cards were canceled. He was even madder when he realized I had my truck keys with me, so he was stuck at the airport and had to get someone to pick him up. My half-sister was at my house with my children and my day care was closed for the week, so everything was going as planned. I knew this was the right time to get everything over with. After days of being in Florida, it was my time to go back home and face the fire.

While in Florida, I had called my dad and told him everything that had happened. He was furious. He called my uncle and half-brother and let them be aware of what was going on. I told my dad to stay near his phone because I was making a move very fast.

When I arrived home, Tim was not there. He had been staying at his friend's house because he knew I didn't want him there. Within an hour of me being there, he was at my door. I had already had his bags packed. I opened the door and told him his bags were packed and ready for him. I asked him for my purse with my ID in it; he refused to give it to me. I walked away and called my dad. I told him it was now time.

My dad said, "Okay, babe, we're on our way."

Tim started screaming, "Who the fuck you talking to?"

I turned away and sat on the couch. "Leave," I screamed.

He ran to me, grabbed me, and smacked me across my face.

I jumped up in his face and pushed him back out of my face. I started yelling, "You can't hurt me. There's nothing you can do that I can't do to myself." Then I played the crazy role. I started hitting my head into the wall lightly saying, "Hurt me, hurt me."

Tim stood back looking scared. I had to play crazy with crazy. I then ran out the front door, got in my car, and drove to the police station. My dad was on the way.

While I was driving, my dad had arrived at my house, and once Tim saw them, he called his friend and took all his bags out the door. I didn't tell my dad that he had hit me; I was going to let the police handle that. My dad had already been locked up. I didn't want him to go to jail for this fool. My dad said it took everything in him not to knock Tim out as he took his stuff out the door. My dad told me Tim was talking all types of crap, and my dad said, "Just get your shit, man, and don't come back."

After Tim left, he started sending me letters and flowers in the mail, but I rejected everything. I was done.

Time passed, and Tim and I went to court. I received a restraining order for one year on him. I dropped the charges. That part wasn't important to me; as long as he stayed away from me, I was fine. I knew him living out on these streets was going to be harder for him than jail. He was so used to relying on women.

Months after Tim was out of my life, I looked into being a private investigator so the next time I met a guy, I was able to run a background check and further investigate him on my own. After attending classes and hooking up with an agency, I became licensed and was able to bear arms. At the gun range, I shot an accuracy of 92 percent. I was now really able to protect myself. I held my PI license for four years, even doing security work as a side job and some infidelity cases.

As soon as Tim left, I filed for an annulment. We had only been married for four months, but the courts said we had to file that within thirty days, so I filed for a divorce. It was hard tracking him down to serve the papers. I found out he went back to the club we met at to work, but every time the sheriff came, he was not there. Then he got fired because of how many times I sent investigators or sheriffs there. I started to get frustrated because I needed that last tie broken.

Two years passed, and I was on Facebook. I started searching Tim's name, but nothing came up. Then I thought, *Let me find his children's mom's name*, and there she was. I inboxed her and thanked her for all she did.

She replied back, "Alexandria, thank you for being so strong. You are younger than me, and what took me five years to let go, you stood up to in a month."

I smiled as I read her reply. It felt good to be acknowledged for my strength. I then asked her if she knew where he was because I was trying to serve him these divorce papers.

She replied, "Locked up." She told me what jail he was in.

I thanked her again, and we ended our conversation.

I called the jail to verify that they had an inmate by the name of Tim, and they did. I quickly wrote down his inmate number, called the local jail, and sent over the court papers. The sheriff received my papers and served Tim in jail. Tim never signed or responded after being served. So on October 28, 2008, I went to court and received my divorce decree for absolute divorce.

About a year ago, I was talking to the same friend I was with the day I met Tim, and she told me she had heard he had hepatitis from drug use and was married again. Tim had three more kids that he just learned about, and he was damn near a bum on the street. I smiled because I got away from him in time. I had stood face-to-face with the devil, and at the end, I was still standing. Anything I had to face after this guy would be lightweight.

Chapter 20

In my life, one thing I try not to do is regret the decisions I make. So far I am accepting of all my choices, even the ones that cost me pain. At the end, I have learned something, and I still rise above and shine, like the best wine, with the ability to appreciate myself.

Oh my goodness. It's months later, and so much has happened. I received my associate in science degree in criminal justice. I just received it today. Wow, what an accomplishment. I am now official. I have my high school diploma and my degree, all within a month from each other. I never thought I'd see this day. I once was a high school dropout and a pregnant fifteen-year-old married mom. I am now a college and high school graduate. I feel so accomplished. I had the best education at first, which was street smarts, but now I have the total package of being street and book smart. Wow, I am doing the darn thing.

My baby boy had his first birthday last week; it turned out great. It was very expensive and time-consuming, but I loved every moment of planning it. Party planning is another one of my pet peas. I had the most fun last year when I planned Robert's birthday party. Wow, what great moments. As I daydreamed of the party bus and the blue dress, I just remembered my whole purpose for writing today. It all has to do with my sister and her husband. I guess they call there self-gaining up on me. Due to this incident, I received a lot of eye-opening information that now has me viewing the little sister, the girl I once adored, and her husband as now just like everyone else. How can someone be your family and turn on you faster than a stranger who just met you? I feel betrayed and devastated. I know you're wondering what happened.

Well, it started like this. My older son is now playing football, a situation I was totally against due to the uncomfortable feelings of being around his father. His father can be very disrespectful at times. And I live my life to avoid all that negative energy. Besides that, we just finished being in and out of court, and my sister and her husband knew of the situation.

When football season came around, my sister's husband begged for my son to be on his team. I agreed because my son wanted to play so badly, and also because my sister's husband and I agreed that he would transport my son back and forth to me without my having to deal with my son's other parent. I should have just stuck with my instincts and put my son in something else; as soon as I agreed, things changed.

My sister's husband on numerous occasions sent my son home by other people besides himself and never even touched base with me to see if it was okay. Then to top things off, an incident happened at the field this weekend where my nephew got hurt close to halftime and they thought he broke his finger, so my sister took him to the emergency room and her husband stayed until the end of the game. I was with my daughters and baby boy at the mall when I looked at the time and thought, *let me call my sister*, who was to confirm us going out later that night. And before I could get an answer to my question, she stated she was at the hospital. When I asked about my son's whereabouts, all she could say was, "I don't know."

I quickly called her husband, who gave me very nonchalant feedback stating he left my son with his father and was not thinking about my son at the time. I immediately took offense because regardless of any incident, I would not break a court order or agreement with a person if I could help it, especially with so much technology as there is on earth. To make matters worse, my sister and I got into a heated debate, which caused me to send out a text to them both that now separates my heart from them. I feel like this situation is a low blow. I never knew the little girl I once bent on my knees and prayed for would treat me like this. I will continue to pray on this matter, and again let God handle things. Hopefully God will open the door and allow us to work out our differences before it's too late.

In other news, the relationship between Robert and me is disintegrating. As I look at my life, I wonder, *will I ever find real love? Or* will Robert learn to understand my needs and be willing to accommodate them. *What is real love?* Real love to me is a man of God. A man who looks at me and sees my worth, a man that will do anything to see me smile and won't go to bed knowing I am unhappy. Real love is a man that knows all my transgressions and accepts them and embraces and loves me for every bump and bruise. Robert is a great guy. But I start to wonder if he is great for me. At this point, I deserve phenomenal love. Love that demonstrates exactly what *phenomenal* means.

Phenomenal Love

Not many people see it because their eyes do not care; they're closed to the world and don't want to share. The one couple that knows it is a dynamic duo that is what you call a phenomenal tool.

They both walk this earth with their heads so up high, looking at each other in the eye. They are not ashamed of the path that got them here; they know without this path, they couldn't know how to love or care. The strength of their words, the love in their hearts helps remove the pain of the past mistakes from the start. It is the tender voice of their cries that makes them wipe away all of the lies. They use the strength of the present to get away from the past. With their arms of hope, full of warmth, they don't wear a mask. It's the tenderness of their love that makes them not roam. As long as they have each other, they will not be alone. They are best friends, each other's next of kin, the way God intended from the very begin. People may see them as normal, but they're far from that. Their love is so strong, you can't break with a bat. Bricks will break before their love cracks. The world may end, but they will forever be one love until they meet again. Phenomenal couple, that is what I need. Phenomenal love, I want indeed.

Oh my goodness, just when I thought I had covered everyone, another shocking turn of events happens. With friends like this one, who needs enemies? And to think I took this person under my wing and mentored her. I know, you're probably wondering what I'm talking about. Well, her name is Ashley.

I met Ashley about five years ago, when her now seven-year-old son, that was two at the time, attended my day care. Everything about Ashley was different from me. We had nothing in common, but when she lost her job, it couldn't have happened at a better time for me and my business. Ashley came to me requesting to pull her son out of my day care because she had lost her job, so I offered her a position at my day care to be my aide. My grandmother, who was my aide at the time, was starting to get weaker and was not able to work for me as much. Ashley gladly took the position, and I began training her.

After Ashley began working for me, we began to learn more about each other. She shared with me about losing her mother due to kidney damage when she was six. Ashley also lost her father when she turned sixteen. And the saddest thing was that Ashley found out a few years ago that she too has kidney problems. Ashley talked about her aunt raising her and how she felt like a stepchild. My heart opened up to Ashley, and I soon found myself opening my world to Ashley. She kind of reminded me of my younger self, and having the feeling of no one to turn too.

All my female associates used to ask me why I let Ashley hang around me. She and I were like night and day. Ashley had a rough demeanor to her. She dressed in very big clothing and old tennis shoes. I tried to teach Ashley how to soften her style and to develop into a woman. She listened to some of my advice, and we even hung out sometimes when she was willing to put herself together. Ashley and I developed a bond. But even with this bond, I never looked at her as a best friend, even though she would call me hers.

My grandmother always told me friends come with years, and I lived my life according to that statement. I knew Ashley was jealous of me, but I tried not to take it personally. I probably would have been a little intimated myself if I had a friend five levels above me. So I just looked at it like some people are made to be workers and some are made to be owners, so we each had our place on the ladder. I sure didn't anticipate that Ashley would totally turn on me the way she did.

So when I got a surprise knock on my door, I had no clue what to expect. Knock-knock. I ran to the front door, and to my surprise, it was my daughter's school counselor. The counselor had come out because she got a report that my daughter did not live in the school boundaries; the counselor had to come out and inspect to see if it was true. The funny thing was I knew the counselor, and she later let me hear the recorded message of the person leaving the voice mail; it was Ashley. I was so shocked and hurt. But that was not all of it.

I started to receive threatening phone calls, with some one saying I thought I was all that and they wanted me to die. And then the e-mails started to come. After hearing the voice-mail message, I knew all this was from Ashley. I wanted to forget who I was and go back to where I came from and beat Ashley's butt. But I knew that was not the smart way. Ashley hated me so much for who I was that she never even knew where I came from and that I once was her.

I began to pray to God on what to do, and God came back and told me to do nothing. For the first time, God wanted me to turn the left cheek without the last word, and vengeance was his said the Lord. And so I did just that. I blocked her numbers, changed my e-mail address, and moved on. I can say there have been times I wanted to go to Ashley and let her know I was aware of what she tried to do and even beat her down. But I know that for me to continue on my righteous path, I must look forward, not back.

I don't know how Ashley is living and whether she even cares about me, but I do know she too tried to hurt me and after all that, I still rise.

Today is February 18, 2013, and I am at my end of my self-discovery. I have decided to end my book. I have tackled the real demons, and everything else is lightweight. Rob and I are still together, but I am at odds where we stand in our future. Being with him has helped me in a lot of ways. In the beginning of this book, I was a hurt child looking for love from somewhere. When I met Rob, because he came off to be what seemed like the most honest and well-grounded guy, I felt I finally was getting rewarded for all my pain. But the truth is, Rob has helped me to realize that humans are just humans. Even with a person seeming so right for you at one time, all that can change.

Rob's personality has guided me to shield myself from dependency. I am content with this shield now. I used to think love was perfect, and since I endured so much, I felt God was preparing me for my knight in shining armor. I used to think Rob was that guy to save me, but he is not in my life to save me. I still have a void even with him.

As time went on, I learned to fill that void with myself. I now realize that no fantasy man is coming. I now know I am my own knight in shining armor. I have fought for myself, I have cried alone, I have withstood lots of pain and been hit with stones, I have stood face-to-face with the devil—and at the end, I am still here. Everything I went through was really God preparing me for a testimony. I am now able to reflect and realize that I have grown too much to allow one person or situation to predict my happiness. I can honestly say I finally found my self-worth, and through my entire struggle, I now know I can only find it through *me*.

A spouse, family, and friends are only companions to help add to my time on earth. The main fulfillment is the one God gives me and the love I have for self. I no longer look for humankind to give me the fruit of the earth because they can't. Anything humankind gives you is temporary. People and life change like the weather. Everything God gives me is real and life-lasting.

I pray that Robert and I survive this earth together, but I am ready to take whatever challenge comes my way with grace. I still have hopes and dreams for a big wedding and a beautiful ring from my prince, whether it's in this life or the next. But God holds the key to my mystery. I told Rob the other day that if he wants us to work, he needs to get grounded with God because God is the anchor of a successful relationship. We will see what happens. If it doesn't work out, I am not afraid of change anymore.

I honor what trials and tribulations I go through. I trust no one. I love few people and care for all in need. As I gain confidence in myself, I walk away from evil. They say you are what you attract. Well, if that's the case, I am attracting success, peace, love, and generosity. I am humble and accepting. With all that said, I am attracting God.

Just think: I was once an abused child sexually and emotionally, a fifteen-year-old mother and wife. I felt lost; I had no one to turn to. I had no high school diploma and no college degree. At the beginning of this book, I was a single mom, dating, attracting men who I now know were a reflection of myself. I was hurt, walking around carrying a lot of pain. I now look at the mirror to the other side of my face and say, "Alex, you are free. No one will ever hurt you again." I have opened up the door that once was closed. I look at myself and say, "You can walk through."

As the child in me walks through that door, I have now grown into a woman. I am a college graduate, the first in my family. I have my high school diploma. I am living without my grandmother, who at one time was the only reason why I stayed in my hometown. I am now expanding my child care business. I am the author of my own story, a motivational speaker, a manager, and most importantly, an excellent mom of four beautiful children.

I used to be so determined to change my name, whether through marriage or court. I never wanted my birth name because I didn't like the life I was dealt. Now I would not change myself or my name for anything or anyone. I never had anyone earthly to lean on but myself, and to tell you the truth, I still don't—and I like it that way.

I now know why my life was written for me. I have gone in circles looking for something that was always in me. I know my purpose and what God put me here for. I feel free; I am free. I may not know what the future has in store for me. But I believe it's brighter than my past. I accept me and all I've been through. I don't judge or talk down on myself or my struggles; the challenges made me who I am, and unless you understand me as a person and my story, I ex you out of my life.

As I live this thing called life, I now accept all I have is me, myself, and I, and it feels good. Today and for the rest of my life, I am Alexandria Nolan, and my pain has a purpose, and my legacy is the words of this book, which will live on forever.

Alexandria, it's okay to walk through the door.
The child can now be at peace.

The woman, the child is at peace.

A letter to the hurt, and the curious too

I started this book at the age of ten by writing down all my lifetime experiences. In 2009, I had reached a point in my life where self-discovery was starting to unfold and I was no longer scared of the demons that had hurt me. Growing up, my options were limited. I was forced on many occasions to choose between hell A and hell B. I would choose hell B, the door that seemed to have fewer bruises. During the time of my writing this book, I discovered I still had demons around me, and unlike in my childhood, I was attracting them.

I knew in order for me to attract purity, I had to release the hurt voice within myself. My journey was rocky, and scary too. Before, I had at times allowed evil to comfort me. I have now learned that I am strong alone. In my past, my inner child was so scared, she kept bleeding on my present. My world was leaking that blood. Each time I sat down at my computer to write, the wounds started to heal and parts of my inner child faded away.

After three years, I have finished this book. It's a bittersweet moment. I can finally let go of everything. I don't want to ever carry the weight of thirty years on my shoulders again. I feel born again, I feel renewed, and most of all, I feel free.

To all that have been hurt, I know your pain, I feel your sorrow, just know there's a hope for a better tommorow. Silent cries go unheard even though you're talking without words. Some people know and refuse to get involved; they are cowards. If they only knew to reach out, they could help to change your destiny too. Doing what's right can help a person's path. Remember: you are strong, and you still can change. You have control of your own destiny, even your fate. You are beautiful inside and out, even if someone told you differently. Do not allow your past to dictate your present. You only live once, and what you do from here on is your chance to live with no doubt. Bring up your self-worth by focusing on your talents; we all have something special about us. Dig deep in your soul and pull it out. Creating on this earth, that's what living is all about. When the going gets tough, and believe me it will, sit back, relax, and take a chill pill. Regain your focus and jump right back in. Know you have a goal, and you will reach it before this life ends.

I want to dedicate this book to Tyler Perry. From day one of writing this book, you have truly encouraged me to persevere. Your movies were guides to tell my story without fear. Thank you for being you.

Love always,
Alexandria

Check on My Pain is my Legacy 2. It focuses on how my life has evolved, my relationship with Robert and what happens next, my mother and where we stand, and my career. Also learn more about the men in my past. Play the pimp, the married man who lied, and much more. Check out the life of Alexandria Nolan.

Send all mail and correspondence to
Broken But Not Damage,
P.O. Box 836, Lanham MD 20703-0836

Alexandria lives in the suburbs of Maryland with her lovely children. She is a successful business owner, motivational speaker, and author; she began to write at the early age of eight years as a method of coping. Her first book ever written is also in print, *Nato the Little Tomato and His Big Adventure*, the first in a series of children's books.

Alexandria is also a member of the NCA (National Children Alliance). NCA helps communities ensure that children are not revictimized by the very system designed to protect them. Alexandria has also joined forces with RAINN (Rape Abuse & Incest National Network). RAINN carries out programs to prevent sexual violence, help victims, and ensure that rapists are brought to justice.

My Pain Is My Legacy is a reflection of a woman's thoughts on life, as half-child half-adult. This book holds the innermost darkest secrets that have clouded the woman's heart, body, and soul. This book contains the key to releasing all the past pains and allowing the inner child's voice to be heard. Every time this story is read, it helps the inner child to finally rest in peace.

Based on a true story but written as fiction, you will discover what a world looks like from the eyes of an abused child whose voice was left unheard. And you will experience the reward once the pain is released.

I always looked for love in everyone I allowed in my life. At the beginning of this book, I was lost. I thought everyone loved and looked at life as I did. At the end of this book, I learned life and I found everything I ever needed and wanted within myself.

I am finally free and loving and spreading self-empowerment wherever I go, and it feels good. Most importantly, my inner child is at rest.